#lifeismagicbook

AVID

READER

PRESS

Life *is* Magic

My Inspiring Journey from
Tragedy to Self-Discovery

Jon Dorenbos

with Larry Platt

Avid Reader Press

New York   London   Toronto   Sydney   New Delhi

AVID READER PRESS
An Imprint of Simon & Schuster, Inc.
1230 Avenue of the Americas
New York, NY 10020

First Avid Reader Press trade paperback edition November 2020

Eagles game photo courtesy of the Philadelphia Eagles.
Photo of Jon Dorenbos and Ellen DeGeneres, Credit: Michael Rozman/Warner Bros.

AVID READER PRESS and colophon are trademarks of Simon & Schuster, Inc.

For information about special discounts for bulk purchases,
please contact Simon & Schuster Special Sales at 1-866-506-1949
or business@simonandschuster.com.

The Simon & Schuster Speakers Bureau can bring authors to your live event.
For more information or to book an event, contact the Simon & Schuster Speakers Bureau
at 1-866-248-3049 or visit our website at www.simonspeakers.com.

Manufactured in the United States of America

3   5   7   9   10   8   6   4   2

Library of Congress Cataloging-in-Publication Data has been applied for.

ISBN 978-1-9821-0124-4
ISBN 978-1-9821-0125-1 (pbk)
ISBN 978-1-9821-0126-8 (ebook)

*For Annalise, who turned my heart right side up,
and Amaya, who will always be able
to have lunch with her dad*

Contents

Introduction

He who has a Why to live for can bear almost any How.
—Friedrich Nietzsche

Sometimes, you find yourself in one of these moments. The type of moment in which how you act actually reveals the kind of man you are. The kind of moment in which, if you trust yourself enough to really listen to what you're feeling, you're able to freeze out the chattering voice of doubt in your own head.

You feel calm in moments like these. That's the calm of inner peace. All else fades away. Your focus is on the *Task. At. Hand.* Gone is the fear of failure and rejection, the "what if" worries about outcome that eat away at us, day after day. You're beyond all that, beyond outcome. You're all about the only thing that really and truly exists: the present moment. You know who you are and what your purpose is. *Let's do this*, you say to yourself.

I've found myself in many such moments ever since I was twelve years old, when I had to grow up real quick. In each, I learned not only how to handle pressure, but how to make it my friend. I learned the power of positive thinking, how to *talk* to myself instead of *listening* to myself. In short, I learned how to build a life . . . when tragedy rocks your world at all of twelve years old.

1

For fourteen years, I was a long snapper in the NFL. It's not a position that gets a lot of attention. ESPN doesn't show long-snap highlights. But the psychological degree of difficulty involved in doing it makes up for its lack of athletic glamour. Pressure? *Shee-it.* Try viewing your mom's autopsy photos when you're twelve years old. Pressure? *Bring it on.*

There have been other such moments. Like when I'm onstage, performing magic before drop-jawed audiences, like the ones who saw me perform during my 2016 run to the finals of *America's Got Talent.* You block out that inner voice that, if given a chance, will tell you you're an imposter. Instead, you tell your story to yourself . . . until it becomes your reality, and the next thing you know, Simon Cowell is telling you you rock and the crowd is going wild.

Let's not forget the harried moments leading up to my ten-hour, lifesaving open-heart surgery in the fall of 2017—one day you're a professional athlete at age thirty-seven, the next you're being told you *might not make it.* There was no time for fear. I had a mission: to find a ninja of a surgeon. "Let's do this," I said to the warrior to whom I entrusted my life.

And now here I am again. Another moment. Just like when a game-deciding field goal loomed, there are no nerves. Just a focus on the task at hand, and . . . calm.

It's April of 2019 and I'm parked outside the Davenport Tower Hotel in Spokane, Washington. In a matter of minutes, I'll be meeting my dad in the hotel restaurant, the Safari Room. I haven't seen him since shortly after his trial in 1992, at the end of which he was sentenced to thirteen years . . . for murdering my mom. For beating her to death in our garage with a sledgehammer and bench grinder. Now here I am, a grown-ass man, and I'm looking at my reflection in the rearview mirror.

Before going in, I need to speak to myself. I need to hear the words. There's a lump in my throat.

• • •

Today, after years of therapy and forcing myself to face tough questions, I know how important self-talk is. *Talk to yourself, don't listen to yourself*, I like to, uh, tell myself. So I walk around talking out loud to myself all day, just like in that car. People think I'm kinda touched. But I've learned the hard way that the more you tell yourself your story, the more it *becomes* your story.

My story is not what I do. You might know me as a magician. Or you might know me from those fourteen years in the NFL, which those of us on the inside of the game like to refer to as the "Not For Long" League, with its average career span of three seasons. For fourteen seasons, giant mean guys tried to flatten me after I snapped the football during punts or field goals. Never heard of the long snapper? You're not alone. You know the guy who kicks the ball in football games? Yeah, that's not me—I'm not that cool. You know the guy who holds the ball for the guy who kicks the ball? Not me either. Not even *that* cool. *I'm* the guy who snaps it between his legs to the guy who holds the ball for the guy who kicks the ball.

That's what I did, but it has never been who I am. Who I am is someone forced to go on a lifelong journey of self-discovery at the most tender of ages. Someone who had to dig real deep, real early. Someone who has spent a lifetime coming to grips with the emotional fallout from one summer day more than twenty-five years ago.

It was the morning of August 3, 1992. My dad had just woken me up. "Where's Mom?" I asked.

"She's at the club, she went swimming," he said.

I didn't think anything of it.

Alan Dorenbos was a computer consultant by trade. But really, he was my hero. He was president of our Little League.

Every day after school, I'd wait for him in our driveway, with my baseball glove on. He'd get home from work and we'd play catch; we'd end every night when I'd say, "Dad! It's time for an American pop fly!" And he'd throw the ball skyward as high as he could, so you could barely see it, a dot in the clouds, and I'd get under it and catch it like I was Ken Griffey Jr. "One more! One more!" I'd yell, and I'd be out there, fielding towering pop flies, until dusk.

On this morning, Dad had taken my baseball gear from the garage and laid it out for me on the kitchen table. He made me cereal and walked me outside, where I was picked up for baseball day camp. I remember getting into the backseat of the car. As we pulled away, I looked back at our upper-middle-class suburban Seattle home. Dad was standing in the street, on the lip of our driveway.

I didn't know then the degree to which my life had already changed. Later that day, I was told, "There's been an accident. Your mom didn't make it." I didn't know what that meant. I kept asking where Mom was. A blur ensued; later, I'd learn that Dad killed Mom the night before in the far-right stall of our three-car garage. And he put her body in a sleeping bag and rolled her up in the trunk of his car. And then he tried to clean up by the time I came home for dinner, after playing with the other neighborhood kids. He stayed up all night, painting the garage. The next morning, after getting me off to camp, he came to his senses and turned himself in to the police.

Good-bye, old life.

Today, when I think of myself at twelve, I think of a shy, wounded, embarrassed kid. Everywhere I went, I felt I was wearing a sign that blared MY DAD KILLED MY MOM. There was so much I didn't know then. Like how much magic, football, and forgiveness would save me.

Magic came first: I'd lose myself all day, every day, in the intricacies of sleight of hand. Looking back on it now, after years of intense therapy and soul-searching, it makes total sense, right? If you're living a day-to-day life right out of *The Brady Bunch* only to find on one summer day a month after your twelfth birthday that your dad—president of your Little League, your hero—has killed your mom . . . well, you'd be drawn to losing yourself in something that could play with your set of circumstances, too: *You mean I can alter this reality?*

Magic became my escape, but football is where I honed my resilience. Every scouting report I ever got, the guy across from me was faster, bigger, stronger. Sports scientists would tell me my knee-to-ankle ratio was off and my hands were too small. Dude, screw that noise. The one thing that can't be measured is what burns inside of you. I learned early on that when life is kicking me down, there's a flame inside of me that stands me back up. I testified against my dad and had to look at the autopsy photos of my mom . . . do you think anything in life will ever be harder than that? Some slobbering dude in a helmet across the line of scrimmage? When you've gotten the hardest stuff out of the way when you're twelve, all else is a friggin' piece of cake.

The truth is, I never wanted to write a book. I don't want to come off like I think I have all the answers. But thanks to some of the very smart, kind people you'll meet in these pages, I realized that you don't need to have everything figured out. The real "answer" lies in the process of self-discovery. "It's good to have an end to journey toward," wrote Ursula K. Le Guin. "But it's the journey that matters, in the end."

When stuff happens to you, you can shut down. You can wallow. You can harbor resentments. You can let it eat you up inside. When one day you're a professional athlete heading into your fifteenth season in the NFL and the next you're being told that you need emergency open-heart surgery, that if you play in your next game there is a more than 50 percent chance you'll die on the field . . . well, you can look skyward and scream, "Why me?"

Or you can be thankful that your undiagnosed ticking-time-bomb heart condition—the same that killed John Ritter and Alan Thicke—was discovered in time. You can feel grateful and pledge to live each moment fully aware of how precious it is. Ever since hearing that diagnosis and having that surgery, I like to stop and say it out loud: "I'm alive, baby."

When you start looking at yourself, when you start digging deep, when you start talking to yourself instead of listening to yourself, you start to realize that the more we can share with each other, the more we can realize we're not alone. My journals throughout the years examine every feeling I was feeling, even when they were painful to look at; in fact, each chapter of this book begins with an inspirational quote I felt moved to jot down in those journals over the years. What I was doing every time I feverishly jumped into bed and scrawled my insights into those journals, I realize now, was cultivating empathy. The more you inspect your own feelings, the more you start to realize all the stuff that so many *other* people go through, too. Life is really hard and there are a few things that are guaranteed: you're born, shit's going to be thrown at you, and you're going to die. So how can we fill all that other space up with joy and happiness? And not resent the world?

By changing our attitude about what happens to us. In *Man's Search for Meaning*, his moving account of life in a World War II concentration camp, psychologist Victor Frankl writes that "when we are no longer able to change a situation—just think of an incurable disease such as inoperable cancer—we are challenged to change ourselves." He cites a case study of one of his patients who was battling depression after his beloved wife had died two years earlier:

"'What would have happened if you had died first, and your wife would have had to survive you?'" [Frankl asked]. 'Oh,' he said, 'for her this would have been terrible; how she would have suffered!' Whereupon I replied, 'You see, such a suffering has been spared her, and it was you who have spared her this suffering—to be sure, at the price that now you have to survive and mourn her'. . . I could not revive his wife. But in that moment I did succeed in changing his *attitude* toward an unalterable fate inasmuch as from that time on he could at least see a meaning in his suffering."

Rock on, Victor Frankl. He wrote that our main concern is neither the pursuit of pleasure nor the avoidance of pain, but rather to find meaning in life. The dude spent years in a concentration camp and concluded that "man is even ready to suffer, on the condition, to be sure, that his suffering has a meaning."

That's what this book is about. It's about finding meaning, in both the tragic and the everyday; it's about how to learn resilience, against all the odds; it's about looking in the mirror and refusing to see a victim staring back at you; it's about disregarding the doubts of naysayers . . . and shutting up the *self*-doubt each of us secretly hears every day; it's about thinking of forgiveness as an act that sets *you* free from bitterness and resentment; and it's about how to ultimately build a life, when, arguably, the worst thing that can happen to you happens when you're twelve years old.

I look at these pages as a kind of answer to that scared sixth grader whose mom was murdered, whose dad was jailed, and who had no idea what the future held. This is a chronicle of how, through magic, football, and forgiveness, you can find inner peace.

Those first two, of course, require more than ten thousand hours of obsessive practice—*each*. The third? Well, forgiveness is more elusive. It can't be obtained through the training of muscle memory alone. But as these pages will show, when you finally feel it—*really* feel it—it's freakin' liberating.

On the football field, there's a nanosecond before snapping the ball when all is calm. Just before I'd flick my wrist, unleashing an explosive force field of violence around me, I learned to say the same thing to myself, every time:

Fire it in there. Don't be a pussy.

It was a way to state my own swagger to myself, and to get me to focus on the task at hand. There were no nerves, no doubts, no fears. Just the goal: *Fire it in there. Don't be a pussy.*

Well, here I am now, about to saunter into the Safari Room. I haven't seen Dad in more than twenty-five years. I'd heard that he'd been released from jail in 2004. Over the years, I'd worked on my own to forgive him. But now that magic and football had gotten me here, now that the love of my wife—Annalise, who I married in the spring of 2017—had calmed me, now that I had stared down life-threatening open-heart surgery . . . something on my journey was missing. I'd forgiven Dad, but maybe I also needed to hear me say that. To him.

I get out of the car. Just like in the tunnel before an NFL game, all around me gets calm and quiet and I become super sensitive to distinct sounds. The boots of the man walking behind me. The panting of a service dog on the sidewalk. The belching of a pickup's muffler pulling into the parking lot. *It's game time. Let's do this.*

This journey to find ourselves? It's never-ending. But what I know is what these pages will show: that if you approach every day with childlike wonder and you recognize the possibility of every moment you find yourself in, you will actually be *choosing* happiness. And when you get there? Man, there's no better high. It's like, finally, you can exhale. It's like . . . *peace*.

That journey is what brings me to the door of the Safari Room, after all this time. I don't want anything from my dad, other than to quench my curiosity—What does he look like? Who *is* he?—and look him in the eye and hear myself say three words to him.

Here we go. Before entering the restaurant, I need to hear myself say it. "Fire it in there," I say. "Don't be a pussy."

CHAPTER ONE

August 2, 1992

When one door of happiness closes, another opens. But often we look so long at the closed door that we do not see the one that has been opened for us.

—Helen Keller

After, people would ask about our home life: *Was there domestic violence? Anger? A lot of fighting?*

You could kinda see the hope in their eyes. They *wanted* there to have been clues. Otherwise, nowhere is safe, right? I always felt like the bearer of bad news. Nope, no violence in my family. Nope, hardly any arguing. At twelve, I was most concerned with who I was going to play with after school and how I was going to make the fort in the backyard way cooler.

Woodinville, Washington, was a suburban town of around ten thousand about a half hour from Seattle. We moved there—Mom; Dad; my older brother, Randy; and older sister, Krissy—in 1987 from Southern California; during the drive north, my pet lizard died and Dad pulled the car over and we all got out and held a somber funeral on the side of the road.

I was a chubby, happy kid, despite the fact that other kids would pick on me. I wore the same pair of ratty old red sweatpants

11

to school every day; the more I grew, the more they tightened and started to look like spandex. In one photo I still have, there I am in the red sweats, a tucked-in polo shirt, and—wait for it—I'm rocking a fanny pack. That's right, the chicks swooned.

No wonder that a group of kids popped out of some nearby bushes and egged me on my way home from school one day. I was a target until that time a group of neighborhood kids was jumping on a trampoline with boxing gloves on. They invited me to join them. I put on some gloves, got on the trampoline, and then a kid started swinging at me. I'd never fought before. But this felt more like a competition than a fight. More like a question to myself: *Okay. We're in this. What are you gonna do now?*

I reared back and took one swing. Glove to putty jaw. That kid went flying off the trampoline. Out cold. Score one for the stylin' kid in the sweats with the fanny pack. No one really messed with me after that.

But even when they did, it was never that big a deal. Because I always had the safe cocoon of family. We'd do everything together; Randy was six years older than me and Krissy three, but we'd work in the yard together as a unit and then all go out to the movies. My parents never missed any one of our games.

Mom would do everything for us kids. She chauffeured us to games, practices, friends' houses, and school recitals and dances. She volunteered at the school library, checking books in and out and stocking shelves, and led a reading club that was popular among my classmates. She *radiated*, man. Every interaction meant something to her. She'd talk to anyone and everyone—cabbies, doormen, store clerks . . . Maybe that's where I get my love for people: Every connection is an opportunity.

Mom was kind and gentle. And always, always smiling. I used to throw a tennis ball against our three-car garage; if my throw didn't squarely hit the single pillar of wood in the middle, the noise would be deafening. Once, Dad came charging out of the house. "I'm trying to work!" he yelled. Mom followed him shortly afterward, putting a glove on.

We'd never played catch before. In fact, I'd never seen my five-foot mom do much of anything athletic. I must have been looking at her funny.

"What, you think I can't do it?" she asked, smiling slyly. "I played growing up."

A couple throws in, I realized she was legit. "Dang, Mom," I said. "I didn't know you were athletic." She smiled. It was the first and only time Mom and I played catch. That was cool.

Usually, it was me and Dad, him sending an "American pop fly" skyward, again and again. As it got dark, I'd ask for one more followed by one more, and yet another. Besides heading our Little League, Dad coached my soccer team. He'd tuck me into bed at night, and in the morning, he'd say, "Where are my morning hugs?" and I'd go running into his arms.

I can remember only one fight between my parents. Dad, behind the wheel of his car, was so angry he went peeling out of the driveway. I started hyperventilating and Mom rushed to bring me a brown paper bag, telling me to breathe into it until I calmed down. Mostly, they got along. We'd giggle when Dad would come up behind Mom in the kitchen, hug her, and steer her off into the pantry and close the door. As I got older, I realized: *Holy shit. They were totally making out!*

Two houses down from us lived the Harpers, Pam and Larry, and their sons, Aaron, Paul, Michael, and James, my best friends. Across the street lived the Witzels, where we'd play Wiffle Ball or football or have intense pinecone wars—nailing each other with those sticky suckers. We'd play a football game in which the ball carrier would be gang-tackled by everyone, at which point he would throw the ball into the air and whoever recovered would be the new victim. Typical kid stuff, right? This was before cell phones or pagers, so my folks had a bell on our front porch that they'd ring when it was time for me to head home.

It sounds cliché to say it now, but August 2, 1992—twelve days after my twelfth birthday—had really been just another normal day. Krissy was in California at Mom's parents' house—Nonnie and Poppy. Earlier, Mom and Dad had dropped Randy off to carpool to a basketball camp in eastern Washington. When I left to go play at the Witzels', Mom and Dad were working in the yard. Around 9:00 p.m., I heard that bell on our front porch ring, and I knew it was time to go home.

Dad was standing on the patio, and I went inside, and he just kind of hung around me. And I remember asking where Mom was, and he said that she had gone for a walk with her friends. And I said okay. He and I played chess; we played a couple games of rummy. We played a computer submarine game called *Gato*. It was way over my head. Really, I would just sit on his lap and he would play it, and I would think I was a really good submarine captain, blowing up battleships from other countries.

Our neighbor Jim Brown stopped by. He and Dad were starting a soccer league and Mr. Brown was dropping off a roster of players. Dad walked Mr. Brown out to his car in the driveway.

Soon it was time to go to bed. I had baseball camp the next day. In my room, I followed my nightly pattern. With two cassette decks, I'd made a tape of the crowd cheering from the opening of Aerosmith's live version of "Janie's Got a Gun." After hours of play, pause, record, and repeat—voilà!—I had about twenty minutes of cheering. I'd hit play as I stepped up to the foul line—a piece of tape on the floor—with a big game on the line. If anyone had been watching, I was just a twelve-year-old tossing a Nerf

14

Ball into a makeshift hoop. To me, I was a sports hero, and the crowd was going wild. If I missed the shot? No problem. Lane violation . . . because that happens so often in real life. A stack of three-by-five cards stood nearby. Why? Autographs, man. I had to sign them on my way back to the locker room after burying the big shot.

Once I'd gotten all those heroics out of the way, I'd climb into bed. Where, every night, I'd wait for Dad to tuck me in. I had no clue this would be the last time he'd ever do that. But *he* must have known it when he pulled the sheet and blanket tight around me.

At 6:30 the next morning, all my baseball stuff—cleats, glove, ball—had been removed from the garage and was on the kitchen table. That's when I remember asking, "Where's Mom?" That's when Dad said that she had gone to the club and gone swimming. I thought nothing of it.

So I grabbed my stuff. I was wearing a pair of blue sweats, the rattiest orange construction T-shirt you've ever seen, and an old-school Seattle Mariners cap. My dad walked me down our driveway to the street, where our neighbor Larry Harper waited to drive me and his sons Aaron and Paul to camp.

My dad gave me a hug, and I got in the car. I remember I turned around as we drove down the hill that was 146th Way. And he was just standing there, looking at us leave. And then he got smaller and smaller. And then he was out of sight.

At baseball camp, for whatever reason, everyone called me Cecil Fielder. Maybe because I was overweight like the Detroit Tigers slugger, and maybe because I hit bombs. Also probably because I played first base—I didn't want to run. What did John Kruk once say? "I ain't an athlete, lady. I'm a baseball player."

I was on the field when Coach Bill Stubbs found me and said there'd been an accident. I figured my dad broke a rib playing soccer with some friends. At the police station, Officer Childers, who ran the D.A.R.E. program at my school, said, "There's been an accident; your mom didn't make it, and your dad's being held for questioning."

I had no idea what he was talking about. No clue. After a moment: "Okay, so *where's* Mom and Dad?" I asked.

As I looked at his face, it started to dawn on me that something serious was up. While I sat there, they called my sister at my grandparents' house, and I'll never, ever forget her scream. It was like a scene in a movie, when you see a phone drop and hear a bloodcurdling shriek. Gradually, more facts became clear. An argument. Mom was pushed down the stairs, which, of course, turned out not to be true: they were sugarcoating. Dad was being questioned.

Randy arrived back from basketball camp. I don't know how long it took before he got there. I don't know if I was in that office for twenty minutes or ten hours. I just remember sweating, I remember my heart racing, I remember wanting to cry . . . but not being able to. I just couldn't. I could barely walk. I looked at my face in the bathroom mirror and I didn't recognize the reflection. It was just an empty face staring back at me.

By the time Randy and I left the police station, the story of my mom's death was all over the news. A crowd of cameras and news vans were outside our house. My grandparents, Aunt Susan, and Krissy were on their way from California. Meantime, I would stay at the Harpers' house, just down the road from ours. I was put into the backseat of their car and told to lie down with a blanket covering me. We drove past the pack of media in front of our house and pulled into the Harpers' driveway. The TV crews were none the wiser.

Once inside, I plopped myself down on one of the two little steps that led into the Harpers' living room. It felt like I sat on that step for hours without saying a word. At one point, I remember looking at Aaron Harper and saying, "I miss her so much and I didn't even get to say good-bye. I just don't understand."

It was the most empty and alone feeling I've ever felt. I'd lost my mother *and* father *and* my own idea of what my life was and would be. I sat on that step because it felt like there was chaos all around me. If I stood up, it might sweep me away. I wanted to bawl my eyes out, and I kept asking myself, *Why can't I cry?* It felt like my body was frozen.

Poppy and Nonnie arrived, along with Mom's sister, who we called Aunt Sue Sue, and our cousin Steve Whitehead. My grandpa is the man, the life of the party, one of my favorite dudes in the world. A couple of years ago, I went into his closet to grab a jacket. And there I saw a collection of caps of every team I've ever played on, from high school to the pros. I had no idea. When it's his time, all I want are those hats.

When he got out of the car in our driveway back then, he pulled out a handkerchief and kept dabbing at his eyes. He went into the house and straight to the hallway that led to the bedroom that he had built above the garage. In that hallway, family pictures hung on the wall. I peeked around the corner and watched my grandpa just standing there, looking at the pictures of my mom and our once-happy family, and he kept dabbing at his eyes with that handkerchief. I could hear his labored breathing as he folded the handkerchief up in his hand and put it in his back pocket. He reached out and took a photo of my mom off the wall and held it up close and exhaled a big, deep, painful sigh while tears streamed down his cheeks. That was it for me. I went running into my room and flung myself onto my bed, my face buried in my pillow. And then it came, tears mixed with guttural screams.

Randy went to stay with the Johnsons, friends of my dad's.

Nonnie, Poppy, Steve, and Sue Sue stayed with Krissy and me at our house while we figured out our next steps. The idea was that we'd stay somewhere for the school year—Randy's senior year of high school—and move to California to live with Aunt Sue Sue after that. Meantime, each night I'd drift off to sleep, expecting Dad to come tuck me in. The same morning scene played out day after day:

I'd wake up to the sound of pots and pans coming from the kitchen. I'd bolt up and run downstairs, thinking it was Mom making me breakfast like before. Mom. It was going to be Mom, and this whole thing was going to have been just a dream.

But it was just my grandparents and Aunt Sue Sue, cooking breakfast. The same scene, day after day. Come Halloween—Mom's favorite—I was sure that, as I came downstairs, the house would be alive with her crazy decorations. Now I know that it takes about a year for it to set in that this person is really, truly gone. That one day I'd wake up and head downstairs and I wouldn't be expecting to see her. But then? I'd just turn around and slink back upstairs. Alone in my room, I'd begin each day, like some macabre version of *Groundhog Day*, coming to the realization that Mom was gone, and bawling my eyes out.

I must be an observer at all times. I must observe all my family, and Randy. I still have to really get in touch with my feelings more . . . I really need to focus on observing everything that's going on, observing my feelings, and put it all together like a jigsaw puzzle.

That's an early entry from the journal my therapist, John, had me start keeping after Dad killed Mom. I'd meet with John—sometimes alone, sometimes with Krissy, sometimes with Sue Sue and Nonnie and Poppy—multiple times a week at a neighbor's house. In therapy, we had what was called a "feelings tree"; it was a drawing we'd make in order to identify our feelings. From the moment I'd walk into therapy, I'd know that the usual rules didn't apply. For example: answering a simply question like "How are you?"

"I'm fine," I'd say.

"Jon, 'fine' is not a feeling," John told me.

At first, I was resistant. *Who is this guy? Why am I here? Why do I have to do this? I didn't do anything wrong!*

From the very start of our sessions, words had very precise meanings. I was told not to call Aunt Susan "Sue Sue"; nor were Mom and Dad "Mommy" and "Daddy." Gradually, I started to get it: Even though I was just a boy, when I was in that room, I had to become a man. I had to realize the issues I was dealing with were very adult. It's a lesson—this sense that language *matters*, that how you say things aloud *and* to yourself can shape outcomes—that has stuck with me ever since. Just ask the speaking agent I stopped working with for continually saying I had "played five seasons." No, I corrected him: "I'm going *into* my *sixth* season."

The agent didn't get the distinction. "But you've only played five seasons," he insisted. It was time for an agent who talked about my career in the same positive way I had trained myself to do.

One day, therapy clicked. I was sitting outside; a neighborhood kid had one of those giant bubble makers. He'd dip that stick into a pool of soapy water, spin around, and form a monster bubble. As the bubble floated higher and higher, I remember watching and thinking, *If I could jump into that bubble, I'd float away, too, and everything would be okay.* But then I watched as the bubble suddenly popped and I said to myself: *Wow. Had I been in that bubble, I would have fallen twice as far and hit twice as hard.* Floating away—escaping—wasn't an option.

I ran into the house and started journaling my feelings—

19

writing them out forced me to think and feel and express all at the same time. Without anybody judging me or even reading what I wrote, I thought to myself: *Huh. That wasn't so bad.* I realized that this guy—John, the therapist—wasn't trying to tell me what's right and wrong. I stopped talking to myself like a victim—*Why do I have to be here?*—and realized he was just trying to get me to put my thoughts into words. He was trying to get this deeply wounded and closed kid to feel and think and express himself. If my heart and mind and mouth could all get to the same place, maybe I'd be okay.

There was, after all, a lot to deal with. The funeral was a blur. A lot of people, a lot of tears. Mom's friend Leslie Moore, our neighbor, sang "Wind Beneath My Wings," but from behind a curtain because she didn't think she could look out at everybody and keep it all together.

The weirdest thing were the visits to see my dad. Either my grandparents or Aunt Susan would load me and Krissy into the family van (Randy was off doing his own thing) and we'd go to the county jail. Wow. Think about that: What must that have been like for them? For my grandparents, taking their grandkids to see the man who had taken their daughter from them? Or for Susan, who was Mom's sister, yes, but also her best friend and sidekick throughout life? Yet they never once pushed their thoughts on me or Krissy. They had to be tempted, right? To say something like, "The hell you're going to see the bastard who took my sister!" But not once. I remember realizing this in therapy: They just loved us and let us figure it out. Maybe that's why we turned out okay, me and Krissy. We never got in trouble. Never missed a day of school. Because our grandparents and aunt respected us enough to let us figure this shit out ourselves.

Yeah, they'd take us to the county jail and sit outside for these odd visits, where we'd just talk about nothing with Dad. We were told not to talk to him about what happened—I guess he couldn't discuss his case—so we'd all pretend that everything was normal. Normal that we'd have to walk through metal detectors. Normal that Dad was behind a pane of glass in an orange jumpsuit and we'd talk to him over a phone . . . about the most mundane stuff. "How was school?" he'd ask. "What are you learning in math?" Or he'd always ask: "Is it raining outside?" As if we were his only lifeline to the outside world.

One time we saw him and he looked like hell. His face was bruised and he looked beaten down. Rumor was that the inmates would load up pillowcases with bars of soap and swing them around on the new guy in the yard. I guess Dad was the new guy that day.

I was relieved that he was separated from us by that glass. Funny, because his hugs used to mean so much to me. From my journal after one of these visits:

I don't really fear him when he is in prison. But I will fear him when he gets out.

When school started in September, it felt like everything had stopped around me. It was like everyone was just kind of looking at me and didn't know what to say or what to do. It all felt very still. And I walked around every day, feeling self-conscious, like I was wearing that sign identifying me as the kid whose dad killed his mom.

There was a kind of somber sadness in the air, in every class, in the hallways, in the lunchroom. One day, my sixth-grade teacher, Mr. Butz, stood before us, as he often did, twisting his wedding ring off his finger and flicking it into the air and catching it. "Listen up," he said. "Here's your assignment. Everyone is going to learn something and teach it to the class. It can be anything you want."

21

Little did I know this was all a front. He'd been, I'm sure to this day, conspiring with John. Because later that day, in therapy, John asked me: "So what did you do in school today?"

Odd. Usually he started off with a question that would get me to express a feeling. "Nothing much," I said.

"No?" he asked. "Any new projects to work on?"

I still wasn't thinking. "Not really," I said. Then: "Well, we've gotta teach the class something."

"Oh, really?" he said, perking up. "What are you going to teach?"

"I don't know. How to hit a baseball."

"I have a better idea," he said. "Why don't you teach them about what you're going through? And what's really going on in your life?"

Whoa. This just got real deep, real quick, huh? I was thinking of doing something more along the lines of how, by the way you hold it, you can put a wicked curve on a Wiffle Ball. But John wasn't having it.

"Jon, nobody knows how to act around you, nobody knows what to say," he said. "I guarantee you, your friends have many questions. I think you can help them. Has anybody said anything to you at your school?"

"Um, no," I said.

"Isn't that kind of weird?" he asked. "Didn't your mom teach some of these kids?"

"Yeah."

"Well, I think they're dying to talk to you, so why don't you help them out with that?"

When it came time to do our reports, I went last. Otherwise I was kinda going to be a tough act to follow. John had told me to speak from the heart, and he gave me one pointer: "When you stand before the class, make sure you turn your hands with your palms facing your classmates."

"Why?" I asked.

"Because that's you opening up, and they'll sense that," he said.

When I stood up to speak, there, walking into the class and squatting down in the back into one of our small desk chairs was John. Seeing him, I felt a mixture of relief and pressure. My palms were sweating and I looked out at my classmates and then down at my hands. *Turn them out*, I told myself, showing my palms like John had said.

"A lot of you know that my mom was killed," I said, my voice cracking. "And she taught a class here. A lot of you guys knew her. That's John in the back—he's my therapist. He's trying to help me. I don't really know what's happening in my life, or where my life is going to take me. But I wanted to stand up here in front of you guys and let you know you can talk to me. I'm sure you're just as confused as I am. But we're going to figure it out. Don't feel awkward around me or like you can't ask me a question. You can tell me your favorite memory of my mom or just tell me how you're feeling."

I looked out at the class, and they were crying with me. And then Deanna O'Hara got out of her desk to hug me and tell me Mom once helped her with her homework. Then came Jared Smith saying how much he missed my mom. And then they were all around me, Jessica Morris, Kristin McCormack, Andy Van Slyke, all of us with tears in our eyes, and for the first time in what felt like forever I didn't feel so totally, awfully alone. My eyes met John's, and he gave me the nod. I know that nod, now. It's the nod I've gotten as a professional athlete from a coach like Andy Reid when I've played through an injury that would have kept others out of the game, a nod that says, *You did a hard thing. I respect the doing of hard things*. And that right there—a mere *nod*—is the highest of praise among men on a mission.

That was my first one. The next day, I wrote this in my journal:

Yesterday I gave an oral presentation to my class and John was there. I cried a lot and so did my classmates. I really surprised myself because I didn't hold back at all. Me crying also helped other kids in my class because now that they saw me cry, they aren't scared to cry in front of me.

My dad's trial loomed at the end of October. I kept telling myself that Mom would want me to be brave for it. And, at John's suggestion, I littered my journals with memories of her, like this one:

At the bus stop this morning it was raining and a good memory came to me, when I was the only kid at my old bus stop and it was raining very hard. My mom said "My baby!" and got into the van and drove to the bus stop and picked me up, got me warm & dry, and then when the bus came I hopped on the bus and went to school. I know my mom said what she said because she told me. And that memory made me shed some tears, I cried. In school I saw a play called A Christmas Carol. It was about Mr. Scrooge being selfish and mean. The Christmas ghost comes and shows him the past and future. In the end, Mr. Scrooge gave money away and invited everyone to his house and was really nice. It made me feel good to see someone's life turn around just from observing his past, and a little his future.

I wanted to be in the courtroom every day of the trial. But that doesn't mean I was going to pay full attention. That voice in my head? Back then, it was busy telling myself, over and over again, *Just get this through this. Just get through this.*

CHAPTER TWO

The Trial

If you find a path with no obstacles, it probably doesn't lead anywhere.

—Frank A. Clark

On the morning of the first day of Dad's trial, we all arrived together at the courthouse—my grandparents, my cousins, me, and my siblings. There was a mob of media, but I found a quiet spot, away from the crowd of cameras and bright lights on the courthouse steps. Aunt Susan came over and put her arm around me and gave me a hug. I looked at her and said, in the most happy and confident tone I could strike, "Where's Mom?" *She should be here*, I thought. *We shouldn't go in without her.*

God, the look on Susan's face. Now that I'm an adult, I think I understand that the worst feeling in the world is when you can't help a kid who is in pain. Aunt Susan just gave me another big hug, and nothing was really said. And then it dawned on me that I'd asked a stupid question. But a part of me really expected that asking that question would lead to Mom walking around the corner and showing up.

Today, being in the public eye is a piece of cake. A few years back, after one of my snaps was a little off and another led to a blocked punt against the Miami Dolphins, the Eagles were bringing in long snappers for tryouts. The media crowded around my locker, asking how it felt for my job to be in jeopardy. *Man*, I wanted to say, *this is nothing. Try being tailed by cameras to and from a courthouse at twelve to testify against your dad in his murder trial.*

You're insecure to begin with at twelve; add to that the knowledge that the world *really* did seem to be watching. The media scrutiny made me feel vulnerable, embarrassed, and ashamed. One morning, I missed the bus and set out to walk to school. Remember that scene in *Home Alone*, when Macaulay Culkin is walking back home carrying groceries and Joe Pesci and Daniel Stern—Harry and Marv—are slowly following him in their van, stopping whenever he stops, inching forward as he walks? The same exact thing happened to me that morning. A news van would slowly follow me and stop when I stopped. I can still hear the tires rolling over gravel, and I remember hearing the van idling when I'd stop. I was, like, *Is this really happening right now? I'm Kevin from* Home Alone. Only *my* mom wasn't ever coming home.

The trial began on October 22. Once, when there was a break in jury selection, I was sitting by myself on a bench in a hallway outside the courtroom. One of the prosecutors, Becky Roe, knelt down, so we were eye-to-eye. She asked if I'd be willing to testify. She was very kind, and made me feel like whatever I said would be okay. "You were the only one home that night," she said. "I'll just ask you questions and you just answer honestly."

"If it helps end this, I'll do whatever it takes," I said.

Inside the courtroom, I was in a perpetual fog. Remember the *wah-wah-wah* of the teacher's voice in the *Peanuts* cartoon? Everyone was speaking like that around me. I didn't fall asleep, but someone would say it's lunchtime, and I'd realize I'd been zoning out all morning.

Still, there were things that stood out. A guard brought my dad into the courtroom. He was wearing a suit. The guard removed his handcuffs before he sat down. Dad looked stone-faced and didn't make eye contact with us. When Hank Corscadden, the other prosecutor, rose to make the state's opening argument, it was the first time I heard a lot of the details from that night. As he went on, I shrank further and further, frozen into myself.

"Your Honor, counsel, ladies and gentlemen," he began. "August second, 1992. Some of you folks might have been out on boats on Lake Washington. Some people might have been watching hydros, some people might have been along the shores of Lake Washington watching the Blue Angels. It was also unfortunately the last day of the life of Kathy Dorenbos."

He went on to set the scene: Randy had gone to basketball camp. Krissy was in California. I was playing in the yard of a neighbor. Mom and Dad spent the day working in our yard.

"About eight o'clock there was a phone call from a woman," he said. "You will hear the testimony. Her name is Jody Lentz. The defendant spoke with that woman about eight o'clock in the evening. He was apparently under the belief that he was the only one at home. The defendant told Jody Lentz he was alone. But he also heard someone pick up the phone. The conversation ended. Shortly thereafter there was an argument in the garage at the Dorenboses' house. We don't know exactly what was said. We do know that only one person walked out of that garage."

Then came the first time I heard the grisly details: Mom had been hit on the head some nine to eleven times with a bench grinder. After I went to bed, the prosecutor explained, Mom was wrapped in a pink blanket and Dad spent the night packing her in the trunk of our Maxima and cleaning the garage. He scrubbed the floor and painted over blood spots. But there were traces of blood left on the floor, the wall, and the Maxima's tires. Dad put the sledgehammer and bench grinder—I remember the phrase "implements of death"—in the trunk, with Mom's body. Next, the prosecutor revealed there would be a witness called.

"You will also hear from a gentleman who is a neighbor friend, Jim Brown," he told the jury. "He will tell you that he came over to the Dorenboses' house that night and the garage doors were closed. Jon was playing on the computer and he was told Kathy was out for a walk. He will tell you that the defendant was acting very strangely. The van was out front; the family car, the Maxima, was not. The garage doors were closed. The defendant escorted Mr. Brown to the door. In fact, the defendant escorted Mr. Brown back to his car, which he had driven to the Dorenboses' residence . . . The next morning the defendant called Jody Lentz again. He then drove over to the King County Police Department with his wife in the trunk."

I guess I heard most of that, but you know what? At twelve years old, while I was living this nightmare, a lot of it didn't register. It sounds kind of crazy to say now, but I remember having the feeling—even then—that this was all going to work out and Dad would be coming home.

When Dad's lawyer, Anthony Savage, rose to give the defense's version of the case, I had an inkling of what was to come. One night, I overheard my grandparents and Aunt Susan talking downstairs. Dad's defense was going to be "self-defense"—I remember the phrase—because it could knock down the length of his sentence. After all, the trial wasn't to determine *if* he'd killed Mom. He'd turned himself in. It was to figure out how much time he'd do.

So there were two theories. The prosecution made it sound like Dad was having an affair with Jody Lentz—her kids were in Little League with me—and when Mom picked up the phone and heard them talking, all hell broke loose. Now the defense was about to maintain that Mom and Dad fought because Mom didn't want Randy taking the family van to camp, and when Dad disagreed, she went ballistic on him—part of a story that, literally, no one else could testify to, not us kids, or any of Mom and Dad's friends and relatives.

Savage told the jury we were looked on as a stable, loving, tight-knit family. But, he said, looks could be deceiving. All was not well—which was news to Randy, Krissy, and me. "The marriage was undergoing some stress at this time," he told the jury. "There was talk between Mr. Dorenbos and his wife that come fall she would go get an apartment and leave him and the children in the family home. Whether or not that ever was going to come about or how long, all of that was brought to a sudden end on August second, but at least there was conversation between the husband and wife to that effect. There is no history of abuse, physical abuse, between the parties."

Wait, what? Mom and Dad were going to separate? "Mr. Dorenbos will testify as probably the last witness in the case; he will tell you that it was family practice when the mother and father got into any disputes, they would go and have them outside the presence of the children and that these were shouting matches only," Savage continued. "But other than shouting and disagreements, they lived as contentedly as a husband and wife can. It will be Mr. Dorenbos's testimony that at least in his opinion his wife suffered from lack of self-esteem. One of the problems between the two of them over a period of years was her feeling, whether deserved or not, that he was on occasion, you know, cutting her, particularly with the children in terms of allowing them to do things, countermanding her requests or her orders, things of this nature. This was a source of some discontent between the two of them."

That's what happened on August 2, Savage said. Mom—who we'd never heard lose it—had gone ballistic on Dad. Seriously?

"On the day in question, she took one of the boys up to go off to athletic camp," Savage said. "There was a mix-up about which cars or which of the vans were going to be used to transport the kids. After Mr. and Mrs. Dorenbos got back from their particular episode, which really didn't mean much at all to him, they worked around the yard. They got a light supper of some kind. He was in the garage. Along toward dusk his wife came out and confronted him with an accusation that in dealing with the boy earlier in the afternoon he had, you know, cut her authority, made her look less in the eyes of the boy, accusations of some kind. And Mr. Dorenbos was, again—I don't want to suggest that was a daily thing, but he was more or less used to this and waited for the storm to pass, and it did not."

I remember putting my head in my hands and looking at my shoes. "For the first time in his married life with Mrs. Dorenbos, it began to escalate to the point where she grabbed a hammer and began advancing on him, striking and yelling as loud as she could," Savage said. "She couldn't stand it any longer. The actions of Mr. Dorenbos will be detailed by him but in reaction to his wife coming at him in a violent mood with a weapon in her hand, from the steps that he took to prevent him from being harmed to stop his wife from utilizing the weapon. And he will in painful detail relate those to you. But as Mr. Corscadden says, at the end of all this Mrs. Dorenbos was dead."

What followed, Savage said, were acts of "confused thinking" on Dad's part—and *not* evidence of consciousness of guilt. "The first thought he had was of his son that was going to come home," he said. "He did not want the boy to see his mother and he didn't want any of the children to see the situation in the garage, which had in the escalation of the fight resulted in bloodstains, articles dislodged, and things of this nature. He did indeed close the garage, waiting for his son to return home . . . The next morning, having attended to his son, he took the body of his wife, put it in the trunk of the automobile, took everything that he thought

might be of evidentiary value, and put it in the car and drove to
the police station, where he, in a demeanor of emotional hysteria,
crying, sobbing, insisted on telling the police what happened the
previous night."

Soon it was my turn. When I was being sworn in to testify, I
was asked to raise my right hand. I'm left-handed; when my left
shot up, the judge stage-whispered, "Your *other* right." My stomach sank. My hands were slippery with sweat as I stared down and
mumbled answers to Becky Roe's questions; more than once, the
judge reminded me to "please raise your voice when you talk so
the jurors in the back of the courtroom can hear."

Q: Jonathan, can you describe the relationship between your
folks as you observed it?

A: I think from what I observed they were living a very
happy life.

Q: It seemed real happy to you?

A: Yes.

Q: Were there sometimes arguments?

A: Yeah, not really serious. Just kind of—

Q: What kind of stuff do you remember, anything in particular?

A: No.

Q: Based on your going back and forth to your friends' houses,
did the kind of arguments that happened at your house
seem any worse or any more often than anyplace else?

A: No.

Q: Did you ever observe your parents get into any sort of
physically violent argument with one another?

A: No.

Q: And did you ever observe them get in yelling or screaming matches?

A: No.

Q: Pretty typical arguments as far as you ever saw?

A: Yes.

Q: During any periods of time on Sunday that you were home, what do you remember your parents doing that day?

A: Normal things, just work and kitchen stuff, like that.

Q: Do you remember any particular sorts of arguments or did anything sort of seem unusual or angry between them?

A: No.

My testimony, in effect, was the same as Randy's, Mr. Brown's, and all of Mom's friends. The idea that *Mom* could be abusive to Dad, that she would come at him because they disagreed about the use of the van? That's freakin' crazy, the desperate story of a desperate guy. I was still in a fog every day in that courtroom, but I knew that everything was building to Dad's testimony.

First, though, there was a different hurdle to get over. John, our therapist, sat Krissy and me down in a courthouse conference room. I could tell by his frown that this was going to be some serious shit.

"They're gonna show the autopsy photos of your mom in court tomorrow," he said. "And what that means is, after your dad killed her, he brought her to the police station in a sleeping bag in the trunk of the car, and they took her out of the sleeping bag and they laid her on a table, and they cleaned her up and they took pictures of whatever injuries she had, to try and find exactly how she died."

He explained that we would be excused from the courtroom when the photos are shown. "But I want you guys to have the choice whether you want to see those pictures or not," he said.

Over the objection of the prosecutor, he arranged for us to have a private viewing of the autopsy photos that afternoon. We'd be the first minors in the state of Washington given such a showing.

We were driven to the prosecutor's office in downtown Seattle, and we sat in this big, cold, empty conference room. Everything was dark around me except where I was sitting. And a woman walked in, and she put a folder on the table. And she looked at our therapist and she said, "I just don't understand this, but here you go."

John sat in a chair, picked up the folder, and said, "I'm gonna walk outside. I don't even care if you look at this. Don't do it for me. Do it for you. If you don't want to look, don't. All I want is for you guys to have the choice. You might be a thirty-year-old man and a thirty-three-year-old woman who may want to have a relationship with your dad. And right now that's a really unpopular thing to think about. I get that. But I also know how forgiveness works, and how the world works. So if you guys want to look at this, you'll never, ever ask yourself what happened. Ever. And if you decide to sit in a coffee shop with your dad and have the conversation and it gets brought up why, or what happened, even if he's on his deathbed, then you'll have seen it, and you'll never need to ask the question. And so it is totally up to you guys."

He stood up and left. My sister and I just sat there. And I reached for the folder. And I opened the folder. And I saw my mom's autopsy photos. She was missing a big part of her head. But of all the major injuries Mom had, I'll never forget the pictures of her hands. To this day, it's not the gashes on her face or the missing part of her brain that brings me to tears. It's that she had little, tiny bruises on her knuckles and her hands. Those were the hits that she took while she was trying to protect herself. I remember paying close attention to the pictures of her hands.

Now here I am, in my late thirties. And I'm so glad I saw those photos. Because I know what happened, and, like John said, God bless him, when I do come face-to-face with my dad, I'll have no questions about what he did.

After we looked at the photos, our therapist knew we needed a release. He drove us to a cliff off Puget Sound, and he said, "Just scream. As loud as you can. Just scream for as long as you want and as loud as you can." And that's what my sister and I did. We held each other's hand, we stood on a cliff, and we just screamed. We could hear our pain echoing all around us. I can't tell you if it was five minutes or seven hours. It felt so good to just scream. To let it all out.

I don't know if John planned it this way, but seeing those photos—if only briefly—and screaming into the universe from that cliff was good preparation for sitting through Dad's testimony. I don't know, maybe I was starting to wake up. Things *weren't* going to be okay. Dad *wasn't* going to come home. Mom *was* gone. Forever.

When he took the stand, Dad didn't look at us. He testified that Mom hadn't been happy, and they were talking about separating in the fall. That she'd get an apartment, leaving us with him in the house. His lawyer asked if he or Mom ever lost their temper. He said he didn't. But when it came to Mom?

"I don't know if I'd be describing it correctly," he said. "She did something. I don't know if you'd call it losing a temper. There were a number of incidents where she would become what I thought was fairly hysterical. She would make fists and lock her arms straight and she would be swinging them all over the place and screaming, 'I can't take it anymore,' feet were stomping." That's what happened, he said, on the last day of her life. She got agitated when he said it would be okay for Randy to take the family van to basketball camp: "She clenched her fists and her face, and said, 'You're never doing what I'm telling you to.' And then she started saying something that wasn't coherent."

Later, he testified, around 7:30, while I was out playing, Mom had another such episode. As I sat there, listening, guilt washed over me. *If only I'd have come home earlier*, I thought. *Maybe she'd still be alive.*

"She started screaming, 'I can't take it anymore,'" Dad said. "She'd stomp her feet. Her arms were swinging. I noticed there was a little claw hammer that we used for hanging pictures in her hand."

Dad said he got the hammer from her, but as they wrestled, she was reaching toward the shelf above her head for a sledgehammer. They struggled over the sledgehammer. "I was trying to hold it away from both of us," he said. "Her head was moving up and down real rapidly and it caught her twice."

He said he saw blood coming from her head. They continued to struggle when he saw the bench grinder on the shelf. "I panicked," he said. "I thought someone was going to get seriously hurt. I grabbed the grinder and I struck her, trying to knock her out." Dad's voice was catching, but he wasn't in tears. Then there was this:

Q: After your wife had fallen to the floor and you had fallen with her, what happened?

A: I swore at her.

Q: For what reason?

A: Because I was furious. And then I looked at her and I could see she wasn't moving. And you could see part of her brain was exposed right where the grinder hit her.

Q: What did you do?

A: I put my hand on her and put my face up against hers, and she wasn't breathing, she wasn't moving. I couldn't feel her heart in the back. And I just said, "Don't leave us."

Dad really only got emotional when Becky Roe cross-examined him, maybe because his story was being exposed. She pointed out to him that no one had ever witnessed Mom throwing a fit like he claimed—and even he, in his statements to police the day after he killed her, never mentioned anything about Mom having a fit or coming at him aggressively, with or without a claw hammer. Then there was this exchange, which stayed with me:

Q: You talked about Kathy separating and moving out because she felt that she was not capable of handling the kids because they were older, and she didn't feel she could control them anymore. What sort of issues were prompting that? The jury has seen two of your three children here. What kind of out-of-control behavior are you purporting Kathy believed she couldn't deal with?

A: It had to do with a sense of being needed.

Q: That's a little different, isn't it, than kids being out of control and her believing she couldn't control their behavior?

A: It had more to do with a sense of the fact that she felt that the children didn't need her anymore.

Q: So since she felt the kids were getting older and didn't need her anymore, it's your testimony now that that's part of the reason she was willing to leave the house, leave you and the kids in the house and move out?

A: That is correct.

Before she was done with him, Roe referenced the testimony from a neighbor who spoke about how Mom and Dad were excitedly talking about Mom going with Dad on an upcoming business trip, and she made sure to get my dad to admit that Jody Lentz was the only corroborating witness he had, the only person he had spoken to about this idea of Mom having these tantrums and moving out. Oh, and when Dad, saying that he took responsibility for what happened to Mom, claimed that, in their struggle, a chain saw must have fallen on her, Roe had had enough: "Chain saws falling on her. How much responsibility is that really taking?"

I don't remember hearing the judge sentence my father to thirteen years. But I wrote in my journal that I thought it was fair. Now that the trial was over, I wrote two letters in my journal, one to Mom and one to Dad. The one to Dad reads:

Dear Dad,

Someday I would like to know the real truth about my mothers death, wether it is now or 19 years from now. I want to know. I also would like to know what was going on between you and Jody Lentz.

I was elected on an 8th grade basketball team. I'm on Aaron Harper's team. Larry Harper is the coach. The team name is the Clippers.

Dad I feel angry and embarrassed to be on the news and front page of the newspaper for what happened. But I also love you very much and am proud to have been Kathy Dorenbos's son.

Love you, your son,
Jonathan Dorenbos

The other one, dated November 2, 1992, breaks my heart to this day:

Dear Mom,

Dad was found guilty, if your wondering. If what Dad said was true, that you thought Randy, Krissy and I didn't need you, you were wrong.

If things were bothering you why didn't you talk to us. Not trying to be rude or anything, the worst thing for you is to keep strong feelings inside of you, because you will get stressed out and yell at people for no reason. Or maybe you have a reason, I don't no. You might get hurt or you will hurt someone else.

Someday, Mom, I will be in heaven and I will ask you what happened.

Thank you for the best 12 years of my life. Thank you for helping in my school (Cottage Lake), being a great helpful citizen to Woodinville and many more things you did to help other people. I wished you could have done things for yourself like finishing college and start your own business. You were the best mother any person could want. I love you a whole bunch Mom!!

> *Love, your loving son,*
> *Jonathan*

The trial over, I remember thinking: *Now what?* For the last three months, everything had been leading to the trial. Now I'd seen Dad taken away. Mom was gone. And both were facts I had to keep being reminded of. Krissy and I were seeing John three days a week for therapy. We had a lot of work to do.

CHAPTER THREE

My Year of Magical Thinking

Right beneath the anger there is a well of hurt. We stay at the anger because it gives us control, because we are afraid to go into the hurt.

—Iyanla Vanzant

So they say that it takes about a year to really get that a loved one is dead. In her memoir *The Year of Magical Thinking*, Joan Didion, writing about the sudden loss of her husband, gives us that inner voice of denial, the one that tells you that reading the obituary would be a betrayal or that cleaning out a closet—far from an act of closure—makes you death's accomplice.

Man, I totally get that. I mean, try being twelve years old and trying to understand what Didion was dealing with. Not only would I wake up every day certain that Mom was downstairs making me breakfast, I'd swear I'd see her face in the stands at Mariners games and her reflection in every passing storefront windowpane. I'd hear her voice in every gust of wind. And then there was the guilt: *If only I had come home earlier, maybe Mom would still be alive.*

When you read about grief, it all sounds pretty simple, right? You read that there are five stages to get through—denial, anger, bargaining, depression, acceptance—and it's like there's a set formula to follow. I guess, in the same way that people needed to know if there had been any violence in my family, they need the reassurance of believing that there's a predictable grieving process.

Well, there ain't none. It's not cut-and-dried. The reality is, you can be in all five stages the same damn day, or at the same time. There are no rules. You can be sobbing one moment and in complete denial the next. You're lost. *I* was lost.

And that's only what you *know* about. You also act out subconsciously in a ton of ways. Before my mom died, for example, I'd never bitten my nails. By the time the trial ended, I was gnawing on them nonstop. I quickly grew ashamed of how they looked—in the same way I was embarrassed that I was *the kid whose dad killed his mom*—but that didn't stop me from biting them, all day, every day. I didn't know how to channel all the nervous energy running through my body. I was in a constant state of anxiety, a feeling none of my peers knew anything about.

One day, Krissy's boyfriend, Robby, came over, and I wrote about what happened next in my journal:

> *Kris and Robby took a walk. Nonnie told them fifteen minutes, stay around the house, they were gone one hour. I was sick to my stomach worrying about her. We got in the car and went looking. Then her and Robby walked in the door.*

I worried about *everything*. Including what it would be like once Dad got out of jail: Would I ever feel safe around him? My journal that first year is littered with reminders to myself about my new reality: *Because Dad killed Mom, she'll never be at one of my games again.* And: *Thanksgiving dinner was upsetting, because Dad killed Mom.*

Randy was eighteen, so he was considered an adult. The state and our grandparents had no control over his decision-making. He went and lived with the Johnsons, friends of my dad's from Little League. As the years went on, Randy and I grew apart. People grieve in different ways. Randy's way was to bounce. I didn't know my brother for quite a while, but I don't blame him for that. I think he was just trying to figure stuff out for himself, and he didn't know where to go or who to trust. We all take different paths. And that's okay.

Krissy was fifteen, and I was twelve. My grandparents and Aunt Susan got my dad to sign over custody rights to them in exchange for not filing a wrongful-death suit against him. They thought it would be best to let us finish the school year with our friends—the following year, Randy would have graduated and Krissy and I would be changing schools anyway.

Looking back on it now, I kinda doubt that was the whole story. I suspect that the adults—my grandparents and Aunt Susan especially—had seen how awesome John, our therapist, was and wanted to keep me and Krissy in therapy for the full year, after which we'd move to California to live with Aunt Susan and be near Nonnie and Poppy.

That meant we'd live the rest of the school year with a temporary foster family. Kathy and Don Robson had lost their infant daughter some years before and had a daughter in college, as well as Jenna, who they'd adopted from Korea and who was in kindergarten. As a result, they were already approved as foster parents; we could move in with them right away. They were super cool:

Today I met Alisa, the oldest daughter in the Robson family. She is a freshman in college. We went to Little Caesar's and had pizza. I found out what room I'll be staying in. I like Alisa. She cares a lot about Krissy and me because her little sister died. Alisa has dealt with death and kind of knows how it feels . . . The Robsons are very nice people. I feel confident they will take care good care of me and Krissy.

Still, moving was traumatic. I was a huge Seattle Mariners fan, and the walls of my room were covered with posters of Ken Griffey Jr., Jay Buhner, Harold Reynolds, and Edgar Martínez. I'd cut out newspaper articles about them, laminate them, and hang them. I guess the adults were having an estate sale and they told me that everything in our rooms that we weren't taking with us would be sold. I ran upstairs and looked at everything on my walls. I remember thinking: *I already lost my family. Now I have to lose my newspapers and posters?* In a rush, I tore them all down—putting a couple aside to save, which I still have today—and threw them out. *If I can't have them, nobody will*, I thought—like anybody *would* want them. I was so sad to throw them out. It was another piece of my old life, gone.

Once the movers removed everything from our home, John walked Randy, Krissy, and me through the empty house. In every room, we each shared a good memory and a bad memory. I cried a lot. In my room, playing the drums and hitting all those game-winning free throws to the roar of Aerosmith's crowd were my good memories. When we got to Mom and Dad's room, John asked for my good memory.

"Mom used to read to me in her bed when I was little," I said, fighting back the tears.

"And the bad memory?" he prompted me.

"That I'll never hear her voice again."

From my journal:

The movers came and took almost everything. My room is empty, and I feel real lonely and angry that my room is gone. It will never be the same again. I wrote a letter to my dad and I felt hurt that I can't hug my dad or talk to him head to head without a piece of glass between us.

Yet, literally the next day, I wasn't feeling quite so warm toward him:

I got my basketball shoes today. They are Air Jordan size 11. I was relieved to get them. My dad is capable of hurting a lot of people. Today's session went well. I feel very angry about what my father had done to this family.

Looking back on it now, in moments like that one and in all those journal entries during that year of magical thinking, it's like I was always reminding myself that Mom really was gone. Otherwise, I wouldn't believe it.

At the Robsons', I moved into a room above the garage and Krissy's room was downstairs, next to the game room. In the living room, the Robsons had an old-fashioned, working telephone booth. One day, Alisa came out of it, shutting the door behind her, and something clicked for me: *She was in that phone booth, a private space, using words to communicate. That's therapy! A private space, where you use words to express what you're feeling!*

Before this, I was embarrassed to be "the kid with the therapist." But now I had an aha moment: John wasn't there to judge me. There was no such thing as a wrong answer. In fact, looked at that way, I was always right. John was just there to help me figure me out, to help me organize my thoughts and express myself.

The Robsons also had a pet ferret. After school, I would take it out of its cage and play with it. You know what ferrets do? Like, *all* they do? They shit. Everywhere. One day, I remember sitting in my room, having heard the adults downstairs talking about my mom: how kind she was, how she always had time for complete strangers; ask her on the street for directions, and she'll tell you to hop in her car—she was going that way anyway. And then

I thought of that ferret. I knew then—and the intervening years have proven—that the only thing I'd ever remember of it was that it shit everywhere. Suddenly I got what "legacy" meant. I wanted to be remembered like Mom—as someone who cared about other people. I didn't want to be remembered like the ferret—as someone who did nothing but shit all over the floor.

As deep as that epiphany is, it's not like progress in therapy was steady. I'd be up and down like crazy. Particularly when it came to my dad. As time went on, I got more and more angry at him, even while I missed him. Or, at least, I missed who I *thought* he was. What I was missing wasn't *him*, it was my *thought* of him, a version of reality I carried around in my own head. Today, when I tell myself *talk to yourself, don't listen to yourself*, that's what I'm talking about: the tendency all of us have to believe that voice in our head, rather than step back and hold the myths we tell ourselves up to inspection.

Don't get me wrong: at twelve, I wasn't some deep thinker about this stuff. In fact, I often lived in a totally clue-free zone. Like the time Kathy and Ed Andrews took me to South Bend, Indiana, to see my first-ever college football game. I loved Kathy and Ed; she was my mom's close friend and he was a big Notre Dame alum and booster.

This was a big game: Notre Dame versus USC. Ed goes to it every year. On the plane to South Bend, I gazed out the window at the clouds, looking for my mom. *She's up here*, I remember thinking, feeling close to her.

Once we got there, we went to a pep rally in the packed stadium the day before the game. During it, Lou Holtz, the legendary coach, said into the mic, "Hey, there's a young man here in the stands, his name is Jon Dorenbos, let's give him a Fighting Irish welcome!" And everybody stood and clapped—for me.

Talk about not having a clue. It never occurred to me to wonder, *Hey, how does he know my name?* It never dawned on me that all this was because my dad killed my mom. To the extent I thought about it at all, I just figured this is what they did—picked a kid out of the crowd and cheered for him. But then the next thing I knew—I don't even remember how this happened—I was being ushered into the locker room, and there, in the middle of it, were what seemed like a hundred college football players, and there I was now, pushed into the middle of the pack, with Lou Holtz's face right up in my grill.

"Hey now, everybody," he said, quieting the room. "This is Jon Dorenbos, and Jon, you're going to break the team down today."

Uh . . . *break the team down?* Huh?

"What do you want to say?" Holtz asked.

I was more than confused. "I dunno," I croaked out.

"How about 'Fighting Irish' on three?" he yelled, while the team closed ranks on me, all hands in the middle of the huddle. Holtz had me put my hands up and start the countdown, which I probably said too softly: *"One! Two! Three!"* And then the room exploded with the words *"Fighting Irish!"* echoing off the walls.

It was pretty cool. Someone from Notre Dame snapped a photo of it, and they gave me an autographed football. Later, when I became a pro, it became commonplace for Make-A-Wish kids or Wounded Warriors or civic heroes to come in and break down the team at practice. When it was a kid, I'd make a beeline for him or her, and kneel down, so we were eye-to-eye. "How you doin', Joey?" I'd say, putting my arm around him, telling him my name, giving him a high five. Connecting. 'Cause when your world has been shattered and everything feels off-kilter, you crave connection. *I was once you*, I'd think. By looking into his eyes and asking about him, by telling him to "stay strong," I was hoping to get across what I desperately wanted to feel, deep in my soul, back then: *Someone cares. It's all going to be okay.*

Because, let me tell you, that first year of grief is really, really hard. There's all that magical-thinking stuff, sure, but there's also coming to terms with what's real. Often, they'd be in conflict. I *knew* what Dad had done, but there were times I'd lose the reality that Mom was dead—by his hand—and I'd think of Dad as a victim and just want to help him. Maybe Randy got it better because he was older—and maybe that's why he had to bolt—but I remember wanting to help Dad even though I knew he was so wrong and even though the anger at him would well up in me. I'm sure that's what was behind my therapist and my grandparents talking to me about complaints at school that I was too rough on the playground. I was the biggest kid in the sixth grade—I towered over the other kids. *I didn't even know I was being aggressive*, I wrote in my journal, but I'm sure, on some level, running through other kids playing Capture the Flag was a way to release some of the rage I was bottling up inside.

In therapy, I started to deal with learning things about my father—my hero. He had a really dysfunctional upbringing; I think when he met my mom, she was kind of his salvation.

When I was six years old, I met my dad's father. He was married multiple times and had been mostly an absentee dad to my dad. He was coming over for Christmas. I was so excited to meet my grandfather. Wait, scratch that. That's not true. I'd been fixated on getting a Batmobile toy for Christmas and my parents had told this grandfather dude that that was what I wanted. *That's* what I was excited for. In came this guy, he had to be over sixty, with his girlfriend—she must have been in her twenties.

He sat down. "Hey, kid, I heard you've been really good," he said to me. I started chanting to myself: *Batmobile. Batmobile. Batmobile.*

"I got just what you wanted for Christmas," he said. *Batmobile. Batmobile. Batmobile.*

And he reached into a bag and pulled out a gift-wrapped pack-

46

age. I tore through that wrapping paper to find . . . a medical textbook. That he had written. Dude wasn't even a doctor, so who knows where he got his information from. But *that* was my Christmas gift. He even autographed it for me. Who freakin' does something like this? My grandfather on my dad's side, that's who. I actually hung on to that piece-of-shit book until the estate sale. Then it got tossed along with my posters.

In my journal, when I wasn't growing angrier at my dad, I was worrying over—and resenting—losing Randy. When he didn't come to one of my games, I hurt for days. When Krissy had talked to him but I hadn't, it sent me reeling. I saw everything from the perspective of a victim; my therapy was about recognizing that, and ever so gradually changing my thinking.

On Super Bowl Sunday 1993, I rooted for the Bills to beat the Cowboys. That night I wrote this:

Still almost everytime I look at that photo of my mom I cry. Why? I ask myself. She didn't deserve to be beaten to death. Why couldn't it be a natural cause, because then I would have thought, it was her time to die.

I hate my dad more for killing my mom. He basically took a big part of my life away and there is no possible way to heal that part. I can't go out to the movies ever again with my mom. I can't play catch with her. I can with my dad when he gets out of jail if I want to. I may not want to see him. I don't know.

Right now, my dad is in Walla Walla, where all the big bad attitude guys are. They're the worst. I haven't felt any pity for him at all and haven't felt the urge to see him.

It's funny, looking back on it now, reading my old journals. I can see ol' John's hand at work, our therapist. There I am, full of rage and fear one moment:

Being an observer, I can picture my dad getting out of jail and find-
ing Susan and my grandparents and trying to kill them and run
from the police. I feel hatred for my dad. He killed my mom and I
will never physically see her again. That hurts me. I really wouldn't
care if my dad got in a big fight in prison and broke both legs, both
arms and a couple of ribs. I don't want him dead, though. I don't
fear him when he's in prison, but I fear him a little bit when he
gets out.

Literally the next day, no doubt prodded by John's leading
questions, there I am, practicing empathy for Dad, seeing myself
connected to him, and starting to see in his story an object lesson:

Today I thought of how my dad's life and my life are the same. Well,
his father left him when he was about 17 years old. My dad left me
when I am 12 years old. {My grandfather} left my dad's mother the
same year and I lost my mother . . . Isn't that funny? Our lives are
very much the same and I don't want this happening to my children
when they are 12, or any age. I don't want to end up in jail or prison
for any length of time.

Krissy was better at expressing her feelings than I was. But
thanks to John, I was making strides. One day, my friend Brian
Kahler and I went to our classmate April's house. She was having a few kids over to hang out, watch TV, and listen to music. A
month earlier, April had asked out Brian, who turned her down.
More recently, she had asked me out. I also said no. Poor April.

Now, at her house, in front of a bunch of kids, she confronted
me. "I don't get it," she said. "You two are the only guys I like in
the whole school, and you both turned me down."

Breathe, Jon. Say what you feel. "My family's screwed up right
now," I said. "I've lost my mom, my dad, and I'm losing my

brother. Right now, I'm not feeling like having a girlfriend." I could see the hurt in April's eyes turn to kindness and compassion. Looking back on it, I'm struck by how sad it was that I couldn't just be a kid and make out with this chick who was into me. But that's not what I was feeling then; what I was feeling was *relief* for having expressed myself. That night I wrote: *I opened up a lot today in front of Brian, April, Kelsey and Marcus, and it made me feel so much better.*

As the school year was coming to a close, I wanted to make sure I spent a lot of time with, and said meaningful good-byes to, my friends and all the people who were so kind to me throughout the school year. One night, Mr. Butz took me to a Mariners game. I opened up to him about my therapy and how I was feeling about my dad—angry one day, missing him the next. I don't remember what Mr. Butz had to say, but the mere fact that an adult was asking is what stayed with me. That someone cared enough to listen about what was going on inside me meant my feelings were worth taking seriously. I remember feeling sad after the game. *It was sad for me because it just might be the last time I'll be in the Kingdome for a long time. My dream is to be on the Mariners and play the California Angels in the Kingdome. My two hometown teams*, I wrote that night.

When the bell rang on the last day of school, a bunch of kids and teachers were waiting for me in front of the school, cheering for me. It was really nice. For a minute, I thought I might cry, but then I saw a white-and-blue limousine—and standing in front of it was Nonnie and Poppy, Randy, Krissy, the Robsons, Brian Kahler, and a bunch of my other friends. Wow! Talk about cool exits. I felt so special. I hugged a lot of classmates and teachers good-bye and then got in the limo. Everyone was taking photos and laughing. We were off to cruise around the town and then go over to a friend's house for a barbecue.

I felt sad to be leaving my friends, but also excited about starting over in California. But there was one thing still stressing me out that I had to deal with before leaving Seattle: Dad.

I hadn't visited him in a long time. Our previous visits had been awkward and left me feeling confused. We never talked about anything. John and I talked about going to see Dad to have a real conversation, an opportunity for me to share with Dad all the feelings I'd been dealing with.

On May 14, 1993, I found out in a therapy session that Dad had sent a letter to his counselor and to John saying that he wouldn't see me unless the barrier between us was taken down. "I will not see my younger children unless we can have physical contact and are in the same room," he wrote. That sent me to my journal:

This gives me information about my father. He is a manipulator, always has to be the leader, has to be number 1, and being number 1 is more important to him than seeing his own son. I feel very hurt, frustration, anger, and betrayed because he won't see me unless he gets his way. I now have to think about whether I want John with me while I'm expressing my feelings and experiences to my father.

So that's what I did, as the culmination to my year of therapy. Aunt Susan, John, Krissy, and I flew from Seattle to Walla Walla to confront my father. Before we left, I spent hours searching for the right clothes to wear. I wanted to look nice, like a grown-up. I wore black jeans and a tucked-in yellow marbled shirt. I looked more like a dude trying to pass for a tiger at a Halloween party than a serious adult, but I rocked that shirt, man. I thought I had *swag*.

Prison is no joke. Freezing cold, with loud banging doors echoing off cement walls. When the door clanged shut in the visitors' room, I was relieved to see that I'd be talking to Dad through plexiglass. Maybe he backed down from his pre-condition; I don't remember. When he came shuffling in, he looked smaller and older than I remembered him. We each picked up our phones and he began talking.

"Shut up," I said, adrenaline pumping. "I'll talk first."

I don't remember all of what I said, but it was no doubt taken right from my journals and therapy sessions. I wanted him to know how what he did made *me* feel. How he not only took my mom from me but also my sense of trust and safety. How, because of what he did, I couldn't even go to a baseball game and not be *the kid whose dad killed his mom.* I cried. He was looking down, holding the phone. He wouldn't even look up at me. There was a part of me that thought, *I can't believe I'm saying this to my dad—my hero . . .* but another part, right out of that therapy room, said, *It's not your fault, Jon. He did this to you.*

I don't think Dad said much. At one point, his head still lowered, he put the phone down on the table in front of him. A guard came over and told him: "You have to hold the phone to your ear." He begrudgingly picked it back up.

I don't know how things escalated. I don't remember if he said something to set me off, or if it was just his disinterest that made me angry. But I blurted out: "Fuck you! I'm the man of the house now!"

He looked up. I could see the surprise in his eyes. "Fuck *me*? Fuck *you*!" he spat out.

"You made your decision," I said. "Forget about us." And then I bolted.

Outside, I felt lighter. Something had lifted. Hearing myself say I was a man helped me feel like one—at all of thirteen years old. In the years after, learning to practice empathy, I've come to see things from Dad's perspective. Maybe, if it was me in his position, the best, most loving thing I could do would be to let my kids go, let them hate me, let them get on with their lives. It was the last time I saw or heard from him. I like to think that Dad letting me go was weirdly an act of kindness, an admission that I'd be better off without him.

And off I was, to California, where so many people have always gone to leave their old lives behind.

CHAPTER FOUR

Do You Believe in Magic?

Life is like a game of cards. The hand that is dealt you repre-
sents determinism; the way you play it is free will.

—Jawaharlal Nehru

Do you remember when you first fell in love? Not the boy or girl, but the moment? You know, that *"Wait . . . what?"* shock of a feeling when you're suddenly slapped in the face and you're wide-awake like you've never been before?

Man, the first time I ever felt that, I wasn't looking at a girl *or* a boy. I was looking at some close-up magic, and the effect was instantaneous: I was in love. And magic has been the perfect balance, the perfect complement, the perfect escape, the perfect ice-breaker, the perfect thing to separate me from the crowd ever since. From that moment on, magic wasn't a hobby. It wasn't band camp or chess club. Magic was *mine* and, in it, I found myself.

Shortly after moving to Garden Grove, California, to start seventh grade in 1993, I headed back to Washington state for a Little League all-star tournament. I was looking forward to seeing my old friends for the weekend, but I can't say I was *excited*. It was hard for me to get excited about anything. In California, I hadn't yet made any friends. See, I knew something other kids didn't know; I knew about loss, and I knew that there was evil in the world. It made it kind of hard to *just be*. I'd changed my scenery, but to me, I was still the kid who knew too much. True joyousness requires suspending disbelief, right? You've got to be fully in the moment to bask in it. I wasn't sad so much as I was having trouble finding my joy.

That weekend, I stayed with my old Little League all-star coach, Coach Bob Schmidt, and his family. They invited their sixteen-year-old neighbor, Michael Groves, over to the house to show off some magic tricks. In their living room, Michael did about thirty minutes right in front of me, and Coach Schmidt videotaped the whole thing. Right there on VHS, you can see my life change.

Michael Groves did card tricks, he made sponge balls appear and disappear from his hands, he lit a match and, when he looked at it, the flame shot up twenty feet as if out of a cannon. I was the perfect audience member, eyes bugging out in astonishment. It was a drastic excitement, the polar opposite of what I had been feeling for the last year.

Michael pretended to be struggling—the old bait and switch. He kept screwing up a trick, reeling me in and reeling me in. I was feeling bad for him. When he pulled it off—BOOM! I was hooked. I thought he'd been messing up. He wasn't; he was making me care.

To me, that's what magic is. It has nothing to do with pulling rabbits out of hats or pretending to saw dancing girls in half. On a very practical level, magic is the art of taking advantage of how much you trust your own visual sense. Most people will believe only what they see with their own eyes. Magicians, however, know that our visual experiences are far less reliable than we think. For example, take a look at what is known as the Müller-Lyer illusion:

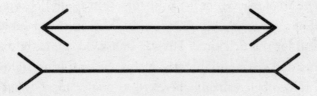

The top line is shorter than the bottom, right? Think again. They're exactly the same length. People often fail to see things—even when staring right at them. Many of our perceptions are, to one degree or another, illusions. My job as a magician is to exploit your illusions by misdirecting your attention, making sure you're not seeing what I don't want you to see.

That's the technical part of magic. It's what we practice ten thousand hours to master. But *real* magic is being made to care, being taken to a place where everything else in your life fades away and you're invested in this story unfolding before you. Think about it: I was a scared, worried, thirteen-year-old kid; now I was given something to be joyous about. Maybe, if Michael Groves played the guitar, my jaw would have hit the floor over his rendition of "Amie" by Pure Prairie League. (Hey, it was the early nineties . . . *every* guitar player did a rendition of "Amie.") But at the exact moment I needed it, I saw a magic trick and was transported. Because there's something magical about magic.

The great ones get it. David Copperfield, Ricky Jay, Bill Malone. They don't do *tricks*; they create a sense of wonder. When you're making magic, there's nothing better than hearing an audience member's sudden intake of breath, shock mixing with delight at exactly the right moment.

That's what we're after, an insight confirmed for me not long ago, after my buddy Paul Tessier and his wife, Natalie, had twins, a boy and a girl, Cade and Kara. I rented a Duffy boat and took his kids, who were all of maybe one year old, for a spin around Newport harbor. I'll never forget holding Cade as his hands reached out and felt the ocean for the first time. He was transfixed, gingerly touching the water and staring so intently at this awe-inspiring sight before him. I remember realizing there are so many "firsts" we're never aware of: first steps, first words. Cade will never remember the first time he touched the ocean, but I recognized what I witnessed him experience: that sense of pure awareness, of childlike wonder. It's what every magician is intent on delivering. It also happens to be, as I learned in therapy, what life's all about: figuring out ways to empty out our cluttered minds and get back to that place where we innocently discover things as if for the first time.

I suspect that, seeing my excitement, Coach Schmidt and his wife took Michael Groves aside and said, "Listen. This kid is really screwed up. You think you could come with us to the magic store?" Because, the next day, that's what happened. We went into Seattle; walking into that magic store was like exploring a new world. I bought my first magic book, *Modern Coin Magic*, by J. B. Bobo, one of the fathers of coin tricks. And I bought a mini deck of cards—ten in all—and used that to practice my first-ever card tricks.

I was hooked, man. Back in California, my room was no longer a sad, solitary place. It was *magical*. I spent hours—I mean, *hours*—learning a lot of useless moves from the J. B. Bobo book, back palms and coin flips that I'd never end up using. I spent hours shuffling and reshuffling decks and learning tricks.

Even today, the most soothing sound in the world to me is the rippling *swoosh* of a deck of cards in shuffle. I've had times in my life where I've felt crushingly alone, at a deeper level than most people will ever feel. But once I started shuffling, I was okay with being alone. And then shuffling made me realize I *wasn't* alone, not as long as I had a deck of cards in my hands. Cards have never let me down. They've always been there for me. For years, when

I've had a big decision to make—what team to sign with, say—I go somewhere quiet and shuffle, emptying my mind for hours. After which—*magically*—my decision comes to me. My fifty-two buddies never lie to me and always tell me when I'm wrong.

Today, there are instructional DVDs, and it's easy to learn a move when you can see it. But when I was thirteen years old, you had to learn by reading. Try following this instruction: "Take right fore-finger 260 degrees, turn right over left wrist. Keep left index at 12 degrees, and hit interior pinky." Dude, that is hard. I would read something for a week and I still wouldn't be able to do the trick.

Making matters worse, most instructional books were written for right-handers. I'm a lefty. Which meant that every time I saw the word "right" I had to tell myself "left"—and my reading com-prehension wasn't too good to begin with.

What kept drawing me back? When I would go into that magic world, I didn't think about anything else in life. Nothing. It didn't matter how sorry I was feeling for myself. There was no voice in my head saying, *My mom's gone, my dad's in prison*. Nothing. I didn't think of any of that. I just literally got lost in entertaining myself. That's when I first started visualizing things, something that would help me on the football field and in all aspects of life; I'd close my eyes and see my hands, completing a trick. Magic showed me that no matter how difficult something is—because, let me tell you, it was really freakin' hard to learn—you can do it if you believe. You know the one thing the person who believes he *can* has in common with the person who thinks he *can't*? They're *both* right.

In addition to losing myself in this newfound joy, I was driven by the shame of what my father had done. To many, especially in the Seattle area, the Dorenbos name was synonymous with a hor-rendous, evil act. I was going to do something that restored pride to the name. That's why I'd dream of starring on the baseball field in the Kingdome and of performing sleight of hand before adoring crowds. Besides the sheer rush of it, I wanted to give Randy, Krissy, Aunt Susan, and Nonnie and Poppy something to be proud of.

Susan noticed this new passion of mine—how could you not? That's when she asked Ken Sands, an ex-boyfriend of a friend of hers, to come over and meet me. He owned Magic Galore & More, a magic store in Orange County. He stopped by our condo one night with a deck of cards. He did a few tricks for my aunt and me, and my jaw must have hit the floor again. When he put a three of clubs on the kitchen table, turned it facedown, and then turned it back over . . . and it had changed to a six of diamonds, I was catapulted out of my chair and went running around the house, screaming like Linda Blair in *The Exorcist* . . . *Are you kidding me right now?*

"Ken!" I said, breathless. "Michael Groves did the same trick! He turned a card over and then it changed!"

If you think back on your life, it's full of influences, right? Some people call them spirit guides, others call them mentors, or even coaches. They're people without whom you likely would have been lost. They're people who teach you not only a skill set, but values, too. Beginning that night, Ken Sands became my first coach.

Ken was in his thirties at the time, with a dark curly mullet pulled back into a ponytail. He was super chill and really quick-witted—in person and while performing. I didn't know it at the time—how could I?—but I found out later that Ken had been having his own troubles when he met me. He'd divorced and had been battling depression. He'd had thoughts of taking his own life. Now he had this wide-eyed kid focused on him like a laser beam.

You never know the impact you might have. I knew *I* needed *him.* But later in life, Ken told me that *he* needed *me* back then. In the same way that studying magic took me out of my head, shutting down that soundtrack of victimhood, teaching magic to me took Ken out of *his* head.

Ken had something called an answering machine. That was this thing back then, in those pre–cell phone, e-mail, and voice mail days, on which you'd leave a tape-recorded message for someone if they weren't home. Because, kids, as strange as this sounds, at one time in America you weren't able to reach everyone you wanted to at exactly the moment you needed them.

A couple of years ago, Ken told me: "Man, you were like that Glenn Close character in *Fatal Attraction*—'I will not be ignored!' " he said. He'd come home and find twenty-one messages from me on his answering machine. Meantime, I'd be waiting by the phone in Susan's condo, counting the minutes until he called back.

I'd spend hours in Ken's magic store. He was always teaching me, but in subtle ways—like any good coach. He wouldn't show me a trick; he'd challenge me to figure it out. He never said the words "you have to earn it," but that's what I felt: I needed to prove to him that I was worthy of the secrets. He'd tell me to work on a trick—"The next time I see you, I'll observe where you are."

What I *heard* was a challenge. I'd think to myself, *I need to show him I'm motivated. I need to show him I'm worthy. I need to show him something he doesn't expect from me.* I wanted to make him proud of me, and prove he'd made the right decision in mentoring me.

Damned if, years later, those weren't the exact same thoughts running through my brain doing drills during practice on Andy Reid's Philadelphia Eagles. X-and-O'ing plays, just like devising intricate card tricks, ain't what coaching is really about. Getting guys to run through brick walls for you—that's the secret to coaching. And that's what Ken Sands did for me: He made me want to prove to him every single day that I could do this thing.

There's this move, it's called a hotshot cut. It's a one-hand cut of the deck in which you end up shooting a card like a missile from the middle of it. I saw David Blaine do it on TV. Ken showed it to me. I spent hours on the hotshot cut; to this day, I can't do it. But here's the thing: in playing around with it for hours, I discovered I could shoot a card real smoothly off the *top* of the deck instead of from the middle. I figured out that I could mask it so it looked like the card was coming from the middle. It was a much cleaner way to do the hotshot cut than the traditional way. I'd found a way to actually cut the cards and shoot a card out of it. It wasn't the hotshot cut; it was even better . . . the Dorenbos Cut.

Susan dropped me off at Ken's store, and I remember running in, all breathless and sweaty. "Ken, Ken, Ken," I stammered, gasping. "Check this out, check this out. I put a card in the middle and then I can cut to it from the center so it's on top and I can shoot it out and catch it, like this!" The card went flying up and back down in a straight line.

I remember Ken doing a double take. "Wait, show me that again," he said. This was me, discovering a way to improve a move. And it was mine, all mine—nobody else was doing it this way. I remember Ken smiling and shaking his head in wonder, like, *Holy shit. Maybe this kid has got something.*

Around this time, I saw the greatest freakin' trick of all time. I was sitting cross-legged on the floor of Susan's living room, inches from the screen of the twenty-seven-inch TV, watching David Copperfield's prime-time special *Fires of Passion*. He brings a woman from the audience—Tess—onstage and sits her on a stool. He explains that when he was a tiny little boy, he wore sneakers that he calls his "Air Coppers." He shows the crowd this tiny baby shoe and then puts it in his back pocket. When he was a baby magician, he says, he would make his friends' rings disappear— only to reappear tied to the laces of his Air Coppers. He asks Tess for her ring. It's a gold panda coin ring, and ripping one-liners that have the audience in stitches, Copperfield makes it disappear without his hands ever leaving his side or Tess's view. Sure enough, he turns around and the ring is tied to the lace of the shoe in his back pocket.

What the . . . ? To this day, it's the most amazing trick I've ever seen. I just loved the whole premise, and the interaction David had with Tess. And the fact that before this trick, no one had ever heard of a freakin' panda ring before, and now there are magic geeks across the globe trying to collect them. I loved that trick so much as a kid that a few years ago, I put out a public call on my website for someone—anyone—who could get me an invite to Copperfield's private warehouse. I just wanted to hold that little baby shoe in my hands. Sure enough, not long ago, it happened, and I get teary-eyed whenever I think about it. This dude, Mike Michaels, who helped me set up a trick in my act, had seen what I'd written on my website.

"Hey, I'm friends with Dave, we're going to get you into his warehouse," he said.

So there I was, in February of 2018, in David Copperfield's sixty-thousand-square-foot Vegas warehouse at 11:30 at night. A magic freak's wet dream, with hundreds of millions of dollars of memorabilia, including just about everything Harry Houdini ever owned. Dave only takes four to eight people through at a time, doing tricks and telling stories all the while. He describes his visits as an aspiring magician to Tannen's Magic Shop in New York City back in the day, and he re-creates the first trick he ever saw there . . . and you're really there: he's transported the store into his warehouse. Here's the original counter, and on it sits the original cash register. What a trip. By the time we get to the Air Coppers, I'm a blubbering mess. Why was this so emotional for me? Because it drew a direct line to that scared kid with a bursting heart in front of that TV at Aunt Susan's. Magic brought that kid from there along to here. I was crying because thanks to magic, that kid—with all his wonder—was still . . . *me.*

What are the odds that a thirteen-year-old aspiring magician would one day be standing in front of David Copperfield for a late-night close-up magic-show booty call? The only way to explain it is to buy into the old adage *If you believe it, you can achieve it.* I think about that kid who followed tragedy by getting lost in the world of magic, and I know that he was doing exactly what actor Will Smith is talking about when he inspires others by explaining the secret of his success. "You don't try to build a wall, you don't set out to build a wall," Smith has said. "You don't say 'I'm gonna build the biggest baddest wall that's ever been built.' You say, 'I'm gonna lay this brick, as perfectly as a brick can be laid,' and you do that every single day, and soon you have a wall. It's difficult to take the first step when you look at how big the task is. The task is never huge to me, it's always one brick."

That's some deep advice, right there. And it was what I was doing each time I sought out Ken for advice or feedback over the most minor of moves. I was laying brick upon brick, man.

By the time my eighth-grade talent show rolled around, I'd become obsessed with another Copperfield trick. He'd take a piece of paper and make it float all around him; then he'd unfold it, and it would suddenly have been transformed into the shape of a rose. He'd levitate it *again*, before lighting it on fire . . . and out of the flames, he'd produce a *real* rose. No shit—an actual rose. I told Ken I *had* to learn this trick for the talent show.

Ken told me the trick had actually been created by a magician named Kevin James, who had a VHS instructional tape on the market. Aunt Susan bought it for me, but Ken had warned both of us: the floating-rose trick was dangerous. It involved fire and flash paper. I remember the word "flammable" was spoken. Aunt Susan said I could work on the trick, but only when she was in the house.

Well, that lasted about two weeks. Home alone, I singed a twelve-by-twelve patch of the living room carpet black. When Susan got home she was kinda pissed—especially when I lamely tried to blame Krissy for it. Finally, I relented and copped to the crime. How cool was Susan, though? "Let me give you some advice," she said. "If I'd have done this, Nonnie would have freaked out. So here's what I would have done. I'd have taken a pair of tweezers and pulled up each little piece of carpet. Just give it a haircut. Just enough to take off the singed top. If you had done that, I never would have even noticed."

Now that's a parenting lesson, right there. She may have grounded me, but she also got across that she was on my side. And it wasn't the end of the world. Remember what I said about coaching? How it's really about getting guys to run through brick walls for you? Susan was a coach.

Our eighth-grade talent show had some dudes lip-synching Boyz II Men's "I'll Make Love to You" and another group doing air guitar to Ace of Base's "The Sign." Heather Wallace and Erin Dodd sang "The Rose" by Bette Midler, and they nailed it. Well, here I come, galloping up onstage. By now, I was an awkward man-child, towering over my classmates at six feet tall. I'd grown my hair long and had shaved it on the sides; in the back, I had a ponytail. And I was wearing a silk shirt tucked into black slacks—'cause magicians have long hair and wear silk shirts, right? Oh, yeah, I also had both ears pierced. Yep. *Killin'* it.

I came onstage to the tune of "Return to Innocence" by Enigma, kind of my theme song:

> *Don't care what people say*
> *Follow just your own way*
> *Don't give up, don't give up*
> *To return, to return to innocence*

I'd once been afraid to be seen as different—*the kid whose dad killed his mom*—but now I was embracing standing out. No one else was into magic, no one else had this kind of mulletlike hairdo—yet—no one else was quite so tall. But it was all good, because, every day, magic brought me a sense of wonder and obsession—much to my teachers' chagrin, especially when the sounds of my shuffling a deck of cards interrupted quiet reading time in the classroom. Magic really *was* my return to innocence.

So I walked out onstage with a candle. It was dead quiet; I could hear the stage floor creak underneath my feet. The music kicked in and I lit the candle, took the paper out, folded it up, and sure enough . . . it started floating around me. It floated over to my index finger; I snapped, and it landed perfectly in my hand. I unfolded it and, amazingly, it was in the shape of a rose.

Now I held the candle to the paper rose floating in front of me. I lit that bitch on fire, causing a huge, bright flame to explode. And now, the climax: once the flame disappeared, there in its place was . . . a real muthafuckin' rose. Excuse my language, but c'mon: that's what it was, a *real muthafuckin' rose.*

As cool as that sounds, there was dead silence in the auditorium. *Shit, I blew it*, I thought. *They saw how I did it.* But then, after that nanosecond of stunned silence, there was a roar and the audience was out of their chairs, cheering and stomping their feet. What a rush, man.

I won the grand prize—a twenty-five-dollar gift certificate to Soup Plantation. Yeah, that's what I'm talkin' 'bout. *Liv-in' large.* Ken was in the audience, and afterward we dissected everything about my performance. It was an early lesson in underpromising and overdelivering. The audience wasn't expecting a thirteen-year-old to walk out onstage and pull off a David Copperfield trick. "I think you stunned them for a moment," Ken said, explaining the silence that initially met my reveal of the rose.

What an adrenaline rush. Until then, I'd been addicted to the challenge of learning tricks. Now I'd felt the thrill of performing. I was hooked. And it wasn't just the adoration from the crowd that drew me in. It was also the surge of energy you feel working without a net. Unlike a card trick that goes bad, there's no covering up a mistake when lighting a floating rose on fire. If you screw up, you look like a dumbass. That's either terrifying or something to lean into—and I loved leaning into it the first time I took the stage. It was what I'd go through years later when snapping on a football field. They might not know who the hell you are, but all eyes are on you. And it's do or die. Do it, or go home. Well, let's go.

I started to study what made for successful performances. I spent hours watching Bill Malone on *The World's Greatest Magic* TV special. It was an annual Vegas gig of countless magicians that was taped and shown on TV. Bill Malone was the featured card guy. And he was everything I wanted to be as a performer. He wasn't some cool dude with wavy hair who wanted you to believe he had real magical powers. No, Bill Malone was all about having fun in the moment. He was a quirky-looking dude who audience members would yell out to, and he'd hit 'em back with classic one-liners. It was nonstop fun, and that's how I longed to present myself. I was a fan of David Blaine, but I had no interest in being him—or anyone else, for that matter. I wasn't about to levitate in the middle of Times Square or push over a palm tree in Vegas with my finger. But what I could do . . . was bring you along for a great, fun, laughter-filled ride.

One day, while I was working all this out, I had an aha moment. Naturally, I couldn't wait to share it with Ken. This was so big I had to tell him in person. At the store, I could barely stop the words from streaming out of my mouth.

"Ken, I've figured it out," I said. "I've got the secret of magic."

His eyes narrowed. *Here we go again*, he must have thought. *More grandiose thoughts.*

"You can never screw up," I said.

"What?" he asked, a little exasperated. After all, there were probably some *paying* customers in the store.

"In magic, you can never screw up," I repeated. "It doesn't matter what we do, as long as the audience is entertained. You can't mess up if the audience doesn't know you messed up, and what does that mean, Ken? It means the whole thing is about the audience. It's not about us, or the trick. We spend all this time routining everything and we forget to see things from the audience's point of view."

Now, that may not sound like some grand epiphany. But it made me realize that magic was just the tool for me to connect to people. I could get in front of ten thousand people and the same move could either get a golf clap or a standing ovation—and the difference between the two had to do with *our* relationship, the audience and me.

It was truly eye-opening, and, I'd learn later, it extends to all aspects of life. Everything really *is* about relationships. How you treat people is how you'll be treated. Put the audience first, show them love, and you'll get love back. Screw getting up and just doing a collection of tricks. Tell an ongoing, openhearted story, and you feel the love, in life *and* magic.

That's what I learned in seventh and eighth grades as magic brought me out of my shell. Now, what to do with all that pent-up energy I'd been tamping down ever since Dad killed Mom?

Well, that's where football comes in. Magic had transported me. Now it was time for football to let loose on the world all of the emotions I'd been keeping way down inside.

CHAPTER FIVE

You Mean I Get to Hit That Guy . . . and I Won't Get in Trouble?

Life isn't about finding yourself. Life is about creating yourself.
—George Bernard Shaw

When I first met Kevin Johansen, we were in seventh grade. It was my first year in California, and even then, I towered over the other kids. I'm six feet tall today, and I must have been around that then. You know that awkward stage, where you're growing out of your body? That was so me. My nickname at school said it all: "Ogre," which the dictionary defines as a "man-eating giant." Kevin had a birthday party, and I was in his living room when I overheard his mom in the kitchen.

"Kevin, I told you, no high school kids!" she said.

"Mom," he protested, "Jon's in my grade. Really."

At our baseball games, Aunt Susan actually had hecklers: "Who is checking this kid's birth certificate!" they'd call out when I came up to bat. "You're going to be seven feet tall and play in the NBA," my friends told me.

Thing is, I didn't *feel* big. You don't watch yourself like you're a character in your own movie. You don't *see* yourself like others do; you *feel* yourself. And what I felt, after all I'd been through, was small, or at least smaller than I was. Later, when I was in the NFL, I'd hear people talk about how big my teammates were, and it always took me by surprise. Because they were just the dudes in the locker room with me. Then one day I saw a picture from behind of me leaving the practice field next to our All-Pro, six-foot four-inch, 330-pound offensive lineman, Jason Peters, and it struck me: *I look like his child. I should be reaching up to hold his hand.*

"You really should play football," Kevin was always telling me. He wasn't the only one. By the time we entered Pacifica High School in Garden Grove as ninth-grade freshmen, the upperclassmen and the coaches were salivating over getting this big magic geek on the field. So I gave it a shot. My first day, something went off in me. It wasn't as intense as the near-hyperventilation, head-over-heels feeling that overtook me upon seeing magic performed up close for the first time, but it was close. It was a realization: *You mean . . . I get to hit someone out here, and get away with it?* Despite all the therapy and all the positivity that was around me, I was still keeping a lot in. Out there, on that field, flying around, throwing my body at other bodies, I was . . . *free.* It felt like . . . *release.*

If magic unlocked my soul, football gave me a more earthly outlet. On the field, all this pent-up emotion flowed out of me. I played linebacker, and hitting guys became addictive. Each time I leveled someone, shoulder to chest, it was like turning a valve that released some energy that had been building for years.

Don't get me wrong, I wasn't suddenly some swaggering, macho dude. I still didn't *feel* big. After football practice and after rushing through my homework, I'd light a candle, put on a Yanni CD, and shuffle the night away. Not exactly Crips-and-Bloods-like stuff. I ran from confrontation and I feared getting into fights.

On the field, I was always a good sport: I'd knock you down, but I'd also be the first to help you back up.

That's because, for me, sports weren't about aggression or machismo or being cool. I've played with guys who were all about the show that way, and with guys who weren't sportsmanlike, guys who would hurt you on the field just because they could. No, for me, it was all about finding myself. In hard-core physical competition, I found my limits—and found I could surpass them.

I started on the freshman team and quickly came to bask in meeting each challenge. Standing over a runner I'd just taken down, I'd silently roar to myself: *You want to roll? Let's go. I'm all in.* You find out what commitment really means. It means pushing yourself. It means living for the fight. It means getting up and doing it again, over and over. "Life's challenges are not supposed to paralyze you," said the African American singer and civil rights icon Bernice Johnson Reagon. "They're supposed to help you discover who you are."

That's what I was doing on the football field. Sure, I was big, but I've seen big guys shrink from big moments. Each time I put on a helmet and met the moment, the bigger I felt. And no moment was bigger than when I was called up as a freshman to fill a suddenly open roster spot and start on the varsity team . . . in the playoffs.

Our team had made it to the postseason, and now we'd be starting a freshman linebacker. But I was ready, because I'd already learned to embrace challenge: Mom's murder, intense therapy, learning magic . . . *bring it on.* At the start of every high school year, the football team had what we called Hell Week: two-a-day workouts in the hot sun, where you'd run ten hundred-yard dashes, eight eighty-yarders, six sixty-yarders, and so on. One time, when we had worked our way down to the twenties, our coach yelled out, "We've got a hundred and twenty twenties!" Everyone groaned.

I know now what the coaches were doing: they were unmasking the quitters. And guys did quit in droves, throwing helmets to the ground, slinking away. While everyone was bitching and moaning, I'd say, "Fuck it, let's do it," trying to rally the guys to tell themselves a different story, to go from surrender—*I can't*—to defiance: *Bring it on.* Even then, I knew I was mentally stronger than the guys around me.

Later, when I made it to the NFL, I realized it's all about attitude. Attitude is the only thing—*and* it's everything. It's your best friend, and can be your worst enemy. Even back then, whether you were a coach, a player, or some hater on sports-talk radio, you had no power over *my* attitude. You want to talk shit about me? *Say whatever you want to say. I promise you, you're confusing me with someone who gives a crap about what you think.*

That's the story I'd tell myself, and it's a story that gave me confidence on the field, right from the beginning. I played well in that first game, though we lost. I still remember the seniors crying in the locker room afterward. For most of them, it was the last game they'd play. But I don't think that's why they were *really* crying. It wasn't the game they'd miss; it was each other. A team, after all, is a family. It could be argued that, my family having been shattered in my youth, everywhere I've gone since has been about rebuilding a sense of family. That's what sport is really about: that Band of Brothers feeling of camaraderie, of common purpose . . . of *love.*

I first experienced that in high school, on my football and—especially—baseball teams. Our freshman baseball team was like the original *Bad News Bears*, and on that team I met my friends for life, guys who were my groomsmen at both of my weddings. Family, in other words. Dudes like Paul Tessier, Jon Fenoglio, Adam Rachlin, Danny Emmons. We all went to junior and senior high together. Danny and Jon met their wives there—Nicole and Debbie, respectively—when we were all in our teens.

Coach Eckles, our freshman baseball coach, was a trip. He had Burt Reynolds's swagger *and* cheesy porn-star 'stache. No one knew what he really did for a living. When we'd ask, all he'd say was, "It's complicated." If he was in a talkative mood, he'd say, "I teach English to Hispanic chicks." Not so complicated, bro.

For some reason, Eckles would show up to practice in a different used car every day. Rather than park in the parking lot, he'd park behind the backstop, where, each day, his ride du jour would get pelted and dented with foul balls.

Why does he park there? we'd wonder, while competing with one another to see who could hit Coach's car.

Eckles's assistant coach, twentysomething Frank Rizzo, showed up every day with red-rimmed eyes; he thought he was cool because he had a boom box duct-taped to the headrest on the passenger seat of his scraped-up Buick Roadmaster Wagon, which did kinda make him cool as shit.

"Why do you coach freshman baseball, Rizzo?" we asked him once.

"Judge said I had to," he snorted. "Parole." I *think* he was kidding.

We had a helluva good team, but honestly, I don't remember the games. Mostly I remember the laughter, and the feeling that we always had one another's back. Just like in any family.

Ah, sports memories. There was the time one of our pitchers, Mike Adolpe, showed up to play in a Yankees jersey and Mets hat. We were the *Pacifica Mariners*—what's up with that, dude? "Son, you can't play wearing that," the umpire said.

"Why certainly, judgey wudgy," Adolpe responded, before adding a Curly-from-the-Three-Stooges-inspired "nyuck, nyuck, nyuck" for good measure. Adolpe was part Native American. His grandfather would come to the games, lay a mat in right field, and sit on it, cross-legged. A couple of times he almost got pegged by a line drive, barely moving while the ball whizzed by. He was such a badass.

Then there was pitcher Brett Woods, who could throw some heat but couldn't always come within a zip code of the strike zone. One time, he must have walked ten guys in a row. Finally, the umpire sent our catcher to the pitching mound with a message: "If he gets it anywhere near the plate, I'm calling it a strike," he said. "I've got a damned dinner reservation."

Coach Eckles would call me "Bush"—I couldn't get him to realize my name wasn't "Dorenbush." At our year-end banquet, Eckles must have had one or six or seven too many. He got up there and riffed on everyone in a drunken stand-up comedy routine. He presented me with player-of-the-year honors.

"Jon Dorenbush, come on up here," he said.

When it came time for him to acknowledge my buddy Danny, I could see Danny's parents beaming with pride. Danny was the youngest of nine kids, so his parents weren't often at our games, but here they were, watching in anticipation as their son made his way to the rostrum to accept what was essentially a certificate of participation from our coach.

"Danny Emmons," Eckles said. "What can I say about Danny Emmons? When Ray got hurt, we put Danny in. When Ray got healthy, we took Danny out. Nice job, Danny. Come on up here and get your certificate!"

Danny got up onstage. "Coach, are you shitting me?" he said, the mic picking it up while we all roared.

"What?" Eckles seemed baffled.

"My parents are here!" Danny yelled.

Another time, I rocked two home runs in a big win at our archrival, La Quinta High School. Afterward, we were out in front of our rivals' school waiting for our bus when Ray Barre got behind Eckles and crouched down on all fours while our first baseman, Brandon Chapman, chatted up our coach. Chapman promptly shoved Eckles backward, and Eckles went tumbling over Barre. But these Rhodes scholars hadn't stopped to consider that they were doing all this on the edge of a hill—which Eckles promptly went tumbling down, seemingly in slow motion. When he bounced up, dirt-covered, cap askew, he came charging up that hill "motherf'ing" us, and tackled Chapman. Our Band of Brothers mind-set kicked in and we all piled on—the squad against our coach, a full-on team brawl in front of our rival school. We smoked them on the field, and now we were reenacting *WrestleMania* in their bus lane. Meantime, Assistant Coach Rizzo joined in, giving Eckles a wedgie under the guise of pulling him off his players.

Oh, man, I crack up thinking about this stuff to this day. But here's the thing. Some may have viewed Eckles as a screwup, but he also may have been some kind of coaching genius. At the time we thought he was just an idiot, but now I'm thinking he was also a savant.

He'd hold pregame practices without a baseball. "Uh, Coach, how does that work?" we asked when he first introduced the idea.

"We are *not* using a baseball," he said. "Here's the deal. The varsity coach is watching us from the varsity field, and he's been on my ass. This way, no one can make a bad throw. No one can make me look bad. It's time for a perfect pregame!"

We all went to our positions, and Eckles, bat in hand at home plate, hit phantom balls to us and we'd go through all the motions of turning the most ambitious, graceful plays. It was like a ballet. We'd make diving catches, throw runners out from our knees, climb the outfield fence and steal home runs. Anyone watching us run around, making plays with no ball, and high-fiving each other afterward would have concluded that the patients at the local mental hospital were on a field trip.

73

But was there a method to Eckles's madness? After one of our perfect pregames, our confidence level was jacked. Why not? Guys like husky first baseman Brandon Chapman had just spent an hour backhanding line drives and sliding around imaginary tags, and then getting swarmed by his celebratory teammates. Was Eckles thinking, *How do I motivate these motherf'ers?* Now I think he was. Because we'd always end up just playing so loose. The game was what it should be—a game. It was effortless and fun.

Eckles would dream up ways for us to bond, like that hundred-degree day when we were working on sliding into second base. Our uniforms were filthy; we were sweaty and *aspiring* to smell like garbage. Well, Eckles told us to go jump in the school pool, and we were off—cleats and all. Of course, he'd never talked to anyone about this. "I was kidding!" Eckles called after us, but it was too late. We were on a rampage. I can still remember the screams of the swim coach and the horrified looks on the members of the girls' swim team when they saw this muddy stampede heading for them in full uniform. But, man, that shock of cold water felt good—coming up from it, there was Eckles, being reamed out by the swim coach. I swear I could see the hint of a smile on his face.

At the time, we thought Eckles was just a crazy SOB. But now I think he was actually coaching. Or that both things could be true: he could be both a bit touched in the head (hey, who isn't?) *and* intent on getting the best out of us. In fact, as I look back on it, my transition to a "normal" life once I moved to California was enabled by a whole host of what could be called life coaches.

First, you gotta remember, though I moved to California at thirteen, essentially orphaned, by then I was never alone. I had my fifty-two buddies with me every day. A deck of cards was in my pocket every waking moment, and therapy had taught me to take note of my feelings. So when it would come—the sadness, the "woe is me" resentment, the anger—I'd bring out my fifty-two buddies and the sound of their shuffle would bring me back to myself and the exact moment I was in. People have gone on treks to remote villages in the Himalayas to discover this simple, true, comforting fact: here, in this present moment, all is perfect—and this is all there is. My fifty-two buddies *were* my spiritual mountaintop.

It helped that I was growing up in what amounted to a cult of positivity. I know that word—"cult"—comes with negative associations. Cults can brainwash. But starting in therapy, and then in California, Krissy and I found ourselves in a cult that didn't manipulate so much as build us back up.

Once we got released from our therapy and moved in with Aunt Susan, whenever I was faced with any challenge, I thought: *How hard can this be?* That was the lens through which I looked at everything: *I just went through eighteen months of the most gut-wrenching therapy imaginable, and you're asking me to make new friends at a new school? Are you shittin' me? Piece of cake.*

Sure, I missed my Seattle friends, but so much had already been taken from me, I didn't even think of moving to California as a loss. Besides, it was a relief that nobody in Garden Grove knew who I was. I was no longer looked at as "the kid whose dad killed his mom." I remember sitting with my man Kevin Johansen, whose dad had recently died of Lou Gehrig's disease. "You don't understand what it's like," he said.

Uh, think again, bro. He had no idea of my story—no one at Garden Grove did. "Hey, my dad killed my mom" ain't exactly a surefire pickup line, after all. So, once Kevin opened the door, I went there, and laid the whole deal out for him. As I went on, I could see his jaw dropping lower and lower. "You lost *both* your parents," he said as it sank in.

Susan and our grandparents were the gurus in our cult of positivity. Every day, you just felt so much love from them. It was like they were there with me in my pocket, right alongside those fifty-two BFFs. I was no longer embarrassed by my story. Dad killing Mom was terrible, but it was also just something that happened. Through therapy, I learned you can control what happens to you by taking control of your own story.

Susan hadn't gone through the therapy Krissy and I did, and I think she was still struggling. She had a tough time explaining to others who these kids were that were living with her. It was a long, painful story for her to tell, so I think she avoided telling it—her way of coping. But one that can eat you up inside, man.

One thing I've learned is the power of owning your shit. If you get caught in a hellacious fire and your whole face burns, you can look in the mirror, tell yourself you look like shit, and go out into the world awkward and defensive about it. Or you can own it to the world—and eventually the world will see beyond it. But *you've* got to give the world a reason to look beyond the superficial.

It took years for me to realize that the reality is, sometimes shit just happens. And it doesn't always have to be your fault. It took years for me to stop kicking myself for not coming home earlier that night. But what if I had? Might Dad have killed me, too?

For some reason, throughout high school, I never went bad. Krissy neither. There were plenty of kids getting in trouble every day—hell, some of them were my teammates—but Krissy and I never went there. Every time a joint was passed my way, I said, "I'm cool. You go ahead, but I'm cool."

Why? Why didn't Krissy or I seek to anesthetize our feelings? I'm convinced Mom was looking out for us, but I also can't help but think that therapy gave us the tools to be honest with ourselves and know what our values were. Plus, we had so much support from people like Susan, Nonnie and Poppy, Ken Sands, and even crazy ol' Eckles, who—even if by accident—made the baseball diamond a great escape and the team a second family. How could you let them down?

I was driven to make them proud and return some positivity to the Dorenbos name. That's why I played basketball, baseball, and football at Pacifica: I was writing my new story. I loved the camaraderie in baseball, but I was addicted to the intensity of football. I was a three-year starter at linebacker, leading the team in tackles my senior year. But the college coaches weren't exactly busting down my door.

I wondered if I should play college baseball instead. A buddy of mine went to Long Beach State, so I visited to check it out. We went to a practice on a hot day. That's when it dawned on me: *Holy shit. These guys are out here all day.* Uh, not for me. Collegiate baseball meant toiling away in obscurity. College football was all about playing before packed stadiums, and I craved that rock-star energy.

So it was football or bust. While other guys were going out and getting hammered, I was in the gym. When I work out, I'm a man on a mission. I like a down and dirty gym. You can have your bourgeois gyms, with their smoothie bars and Pilates classes. I want to pump iron—and I want to do it alone. I'd hit the gym every day, bench-pressing 225 pounds with the sounds of Metallica pounding around my brain.

Silently, I'd talk to all those college scouts who weren't coming to my games. With each lift, I'd exhale the phrase: *I am Division One!* Or: *Go ahead. Pour some gasoline on my fire.*

There were no takers, which was okay. It is what it is. It was the first of many times the so-called smart money would bet against me. *Too small. Too slow. Not athletic.* What they didn't know was the power of the beats in my chest. But they would, I'd make certain of that.

How? By following my buddy and high school teammate Paul

Tessier's lead and attending Golden West Junior College in Huntington Beach. The Golden West football Rustlers—a nickname to strike fear in the hearts of animal and man alike—had posted precisely zero wins in their last thirty games. They barely had enough players to field a team. The left tackle pulled double duty as the punter—no doubt the biggest punter in the history of the game. To me, it sounded perfect. A school in need of a turnaround. I knew all about comebacks. Besides, as I flipped through the Golden West brochure, there was this thought: *If I can't play here, I won't play anywhere.*

CHAPTER SIX

How Pamela Anderson's Porn Tape Made Me a Long Snapper

Happy are those who dream dreams and are ready to pay the price to make them come true.

—Leon Joseph Suenens

Here comes Jonny. Every day at Golden West, I'd roll up to practice in my Ford F-150, named Beastie, cranking "Cowboy" by Kid Rock:

Buy a yacht with a flag sayin' "chillin' the most"
Then rock that bitch up and down the coast . . .

I'd tell myself back then I was a badass. I was hitting the weight room every day and felt jacked. Who knows, maybe I looked like Pee-wee Herman, but what's important is that I was living my swagger—and that meant I was pulling it off. I'd get out of that truck in a cutoff tee, wearing a tight cowboy hat, Kid Rock blaring, and saunter onto the field: *Let's do this.*

That wasn't *me*, or at least it wasn't all of me. I'd adopted a character. A kind of alter ego—the part of you that does what you do on the football field. To aspire to be the best at something, that's what you do. You give birth to a whole different part of yourself. Now, my character creation was pretty tame. I didn't go nearly as far as some.

For example, when I became a Philadelphia Eagle in 2006 and first walked into that locker room, I saw a murderer's row of lockers: McNabb. Trotter. Westbrook. Dawkins. Weapon X. Wait . . . Weapon X? Who was that? And why did his locker have all these little figurines and dolls in it?

Well, Weapon X was future Hall of Famer Brian Dawkins's other personality. The dude's ferocious game-day alter ego had its own freakin' locker. Crazy, right? But I came to see it as making perfect sense. You want to be that good at something? You don't study it. You *become* it. You instill that confidence in yourself. We become who we project ourselves to be.

In order for Dawkins to perform at the emotional and physical heights he did week in and week out for sixteen years, he had to create a persona. I've played with other guys of otherworldly talent who have all done the same, in part because it's the only way they can understand how they do what they do. In interviews, they talk about their "game" in the third person, as if it's something that lives separate and apart from them. That's because it does. During the week, Brian Dawkins was a civilized member of society: nice guy, with a wife and kids. Come Sunday, he was Weapon X, the ultimate soldier and a dude I wouldn't want to run into in a dark alley.

Of course, at Golden West, I didn't exactly back up my macho strut with a Dawkins-like level of play. But each day I was learning. In high school, I found my way to the ball and hit guys. I didn't know what a pulling guard was or even what zone coverage was. I just flew to the ball.

But now, because we had only just enough guys to field a full team on both sides of the ball, practice became the ultimate classroom for me. At times, it seemed like we needed everybody healthy or we'd have to forfeit. That meant we'd have limited contact at practice. Not only that, during some drills we would barely even run. Coach Joe Hay would clap, and you'd have to step your feet to his clap in slow motion. His clap was the metronome to which we walked through all our plays.

For me, it was genius. Because the game was slowed down, literally step-by-step, I was starting to see it unfold in real time. All those things I shrugged off before—like whoever that "pulling guard" was—now I saw, and saw how to react. Turns out, when you slowly walk through the game, there are no false steps, there's no overthinking, there's no hesitation, there's no second-guessing. Every step is right where you're supposed to be. You start visualizing the game unfolding in front of you. Football without running and hitting was like Coach Eckles's pregame workouts without the ball, all over again.

How perfect was this for me? My whole life, after all, was all about visualization, about seeing in your head who you want to be and then realizing the dream. Now I was doing the same thing on the football field. When special-teams practice at full speed with hitting, it's really just a bunch of idiots flying around and putting themselves in danger. From then on, walk-throughs were how I learned.

You wouldn't know it from our record—we were oh-and-ten in what turned out to be my only season at Golden West—but Coach Hay was a great coach who loved making a positive impact on young men's lives. He was a big, strong, energetic dude who worked out like a fiend, but who tragically died in 2012 of sleep apnea at just forty-one years old. I doubt I would have made it to the NFL without what I learned from him.

He was a master motivator. One day he asked us, "Why do we play this game?"

"Uh, we play to win," someone called out.

"Nope," he said. "That's not why we play."

Hmm. Silence. Now, a team of meatheads were all looking at their feet, dumbfounded. We weren't exactly a scholarly bunch. Like many a junior college program, we had our share of screwups and delinquents, and even some ex-cons, guys in their midtwenties looking to make good on a second chance. We were one dim-witted crew, suddenly stumped by a simple question: Why *did* we play this game?

"You play for one reason and one reason only," Coach Hay said, trying to prompt us.

Still more silence. Finally someone spoke up: "Coach, you're going to have to tell us. We don't have a clue."

Coach Hay opened a can o' wisdom on us. "You play to become the teammate that your teammates will hate to lose and that your opponents will fear," he said. "If you work so hard that you become *that* teammate, the one your brothers need, and the one who every opponent respects—then I promise you, you will win more than you lose. We know we ain't winning every game. But if you lose, you want that guy you went against to walk across the field and look at you and say, 'You are the toughest motherfucker I've ever lined up against.' If you have his respect, you'll win more than you lose. And, gentlemen, that will go far beyond the game. That's a life lesson."

Man, I was jacked. I loved Coach Hay's Knute Rockne–like talks to the team, even when he made fun of me. One day, he asked us, "Why are your names on the back of your jerseys?"

Genius over here shot up his hand. "I know, Coach," I said. "There are a lot of guys out here, so if you don't know someone's name, you can look at his jersey and call him by his name when you talk to him and that'll make him feel good, and maybe he'll train harder because he'll think you care about him."

Hay just looked at me. I think he was kinda stunned. "That's the stupidest answer I've ever heard," he said, prompting all the other deep thinkers to crack up. Then Coach Hay got serious.

"I actually think it's pretty simple," he said. "Everything that happens in life is going to happen between those white lines on the field. Everything—how you get up, whether you help your brother, whether you bitch and moan—is a direct reflection of who you are. That's the person you're bringing to this world. And you can't hide from it."

Some teams—like, famously, Joe Paterno's Penn State—purposely sent players out on the field without their names on their jerseys. The idea was to reject individual ego: team trumps all. Hay wasn't having any of it.

"I'm all for having your name on that jersey, because it holds you accountable," he said. "Everything you experience in this game is gonna happen to you in life. You're gonna fuck up, you're gonna be called out, you're gonna score touchdowns, you're gonna fumble, you're gonna have big hits, you're gonna get hit, you're gonna break bones, you're gonna let people down, people are gonna let you down. But ultimately, how you react to all that within those white lines? That's who you're going to be as a person. Are you going to be a whiny little bitch who points fingers and doesn't take responsibility, or are you gonna be someone who helps up a fallen teammate? People will look at that name and know from how you respond to everything that happens to you what kind of man you are."

Whoa. We were just laughing (at me), and now we'd gone real deep. That's how Coach Hay was—he had a way of saying things that made you want to be a better person. One time, we were running lines—running from one side of the field to the other, touching the white sideline, and running back. Coach Hay stopped us, mid-drill.

"Hey, you guys want to know why we haven't won a game?" he said. "'Cause you don't take care of the small things. I tell you to run to the white line and touch the white line, and yet half of you guys come up four inches short. You're never gonna achieve the big thing if you let all the little things slip. You might not think that four inches is that big a deal, but eventually those four inches catch up to you. Years from now, you're gonna fall short of something really important in your life, and you're gonna wonder why. It'll be because you learned to settle. You accepted coming up just a little short. If you do the little things right, I promise you the big things will come. But only if you hold yourself to the highest standard."

Coach Hay's warning stayed with me. Years later, after I became a pro, I got the bright idea to take flying lessons. I've always felt closer to my mom when I'm in the sky, and I'd always thought about the song her friend Leslie Moore sang at her funeral: "The Wind Beneath My Wings," and particularly the line "*I could fly higher than an eagle.*" So there I was, in the cockpit, and my flight instructor, Reed, was telling me to hold the plane at ten thousand feet.

"I am," I said.

"No, you're not," Reed said. "You're holding at ten thousand and twenty-five feet."

When we landed, Reed pulled me aside. "Look, man, it doesn't really matter to me," he said. "But if I tell you to hold at ten thousand feet, hold at ten thousand feet. Because if you're going to settle for fifteen feet here and fifteen feet there, you're going to settle everywhere in life, and I know you—you're not that guy. So do it for yourself—have a higher standard for who you are."

I must have been ten years removed from that Golden West locker room, but it hit me: *Coach Hay, you muthafucka, you were so damned right.* Now I see his message everywhere. On the wall of their state-of-the-art training facility, the San Antonio Spurs have this quote prominently displayed, and it makes me smile, think of Coach Hay, and send a high five skyward:

> When nothing seems to help, I go look at a stonecutter hammering away at his rock perhaps a hundred times without as much as a crack showing in it. Yet at the hundred and first blow it will split in two, and I know it was not that blow that did it, but all that had gone before.
>
> —Jacob Riis

What Coach Hay knew—and, no doubt, what Spurs Coach Gregg Popovich knows—is that losing hurts more than winning feels good. It's unacceptable to be the weakest link in the chain, so how do you avoid that? By the steady application of principle, which is a lesson that extends well beyond sports. That was the point of retired US Admiral William McRaven's commencement speech a couple of years ago that went viral and eventually turned into a book, *Make Your Bed: Little Things Can Change Your Life . . . and Maybe the World.*

"If you make your bed every morning, you will have accomplished the first task of the day," McRaven told University of Texas at Austin students in 2014, in a speech I memorized. "It will give you a small sense of pride, and it will encourage you to do another task, and another, and another. And by the end of the day that one task completed will have turned into many tasks completed."

Of course, none of this wisdom helped us on the field at Golden West. We were terrible. We had a lot of great athletes, but we lacked discipline. In fact, our last game of the season kind of captured the whole year. It was at Riverside City College, and they scored in the last ten seconds to beat us. Then, during their celebration, their team and fans started chanting, *"Oh-and-ten! Oh-and-ten!"*

Well, a bunch of guys on our team had done prison time. You could beat us on the field, but disrespect us? Now you've violated prison rules. So some of our goon teammates led the charge and we had a full, bench-clearing brawl to end our season. I looked at Brett Woods, who'd come to Golden West with me from high school, and we had a moment before following our rampaging teammates into the scrum.

"We just got our ass kicked in the game and now we've gotta get our ass kicked in a fight," Brett said.

"Getting our ass kicked twice in one night," I said. "That's not a good day."

With that, we ran out there and tried to look angry, moving around, trying like hell to avoid anything that could, like, hurt. (Can we just pause for a moment to acknowledge how dumb fighting in football is? Guys trying to punch guys in the face who are *wearing helmets*? Seriously?)

After that debacle, I revisited my Division I dream. I loved Coach Hay, but thought, *I've gotta get outta here.* My academics were solid enough that I could be eligible right away for a major program. The problem was that not a whole helluva lot of college scouts were coming to see this winless team. So I hatched a plan.

First, I got back in the weight room, for hours at a time. Instead of listening to that inner voice of doubt—"No one from an oh-and-ten juco can make it to the big time"—you could find me every day on a bench press, grunting "I *am* Division One!" with every rep, telling myself the story I needed to hear.

The more I thought about it, the clearer it became to me that long snapping was my ticket to realizing my dream of playing before a stadium of a hundred thousand screaming fans. I had snapped my senior year of high school, and I fooled around with it during practice at Golden West. I didn't really know how to do it, but I knew I had a knack for it. I could get the ball back to the punter or holder in a serious hurry, even if I had no clue where it would end up.

Today, there are actually camps just for long snappers. I can't believe there are fourteen-year-olds out there who dream about nothing else but snapping, but apparently there are. The snappers who make it to the NFL share many of the same traits. They're all extremely comfortable in that awkward position, and they can generate power out of it without falling forward, which creates a pendulum effect and causes the ball to sail high. For whatever reason, I'm really flexible. I can do splits and can squat like a catcher. The trick is generating power while staying square and flat-footed, like you're seated in a chair, maintaining your balance while some drooling idiot is trying to knock you on your ass.

There's no natural torque to the motion of snapping, so the force has to come from your hips, hamstrings, back, and shoulders, all while sliding backward. Back then, in the weight room, I knew none of this. What I knew was that, when I bent over the ball and snapped it between my legs backward, it sizzled through the air and would land in a punter's hands—*if* it was on target— with a loud *thud*.

Yep, snapping would be my ticket. My high school teammate Paul Tessier, who I'd followed to Golden West, was now at the University of Texas at El Paso (UTEP). "Dude, we're looking for a snapper," he told me.

There was only one problem: I had no videotape of me snapping. But thank God for Pamela Anderson's sex tape. See, back in the pre-Internet, pre-high-definition days of videotape and VCRs, you could get a bootlegged tape and splice together a copy of it, using two VCRs. A bunch of us grew very adept at this art when Pamela Anderson's sex tape started making the rounds. Everyone wanted one.

Well, it was time to put this talent to good use. I went to Coach Hay and asked if he could loan me some game tape. There was our long snapper, Tim Thurman. Tim was six-foot-six, and better *then* than I ever was. Another teammate was Nick Heinle; like me, he played linebacker and defensive end. Nick wore number 48 and I was number 47. We were both white and built roughly similar, but Nick hit way harder than I did. He was an animal.

We were kind of an odd couple, Nick and I, the meathead and the sensitive guy. One day, Coach Hay asked, "Dorenbos, what did you do this weekend?"

"I watched the movie *Notting Hill*, Coach," I said. "It stars Julia Roberts and Hugh Grant—"

"Jesus," Hay said, cutting me off, "are you shitting me? Heinle, what'd you do?"

"I stayed home and watched *Braveheart*, sir," Nick said.

"Hell yeah, you did," Hay said. "Dorenbos, go to the movies more often with Heinle."

Anyway, once I got tape of Nick's big hits from Coach Hay, I spliced together a highlight reel of some of my plays, Nick's biggest hits, and Tim's best snaps, and passed it off as my own. Sure, Tim was six-six, but these were the days of grainy video footage. No one would notice that in some plays I was six inches taller, right?

Yeah, that's right, you could say I conned my way to a full scholarship for a position I never really played. But I knew I could do it; I just needed the opportunity. Tessier thought I was a stone-cold lunatic. "You did *what*?" he screamed when I told him I'd sent the tape to his coaches.

Feel free to judge me for how I got my scholarship. Yes, it was, on one level, dishonest. But what I learned growing up, going through what I'd gone through, led me not to give a fuck—and it was liberating. I had no fear, which is, by the way, precisely the character trait you want in your long snapper.

Besides, by now I'd seen that who gets a free ride, just as who gets an NFL roster spot, can be totally political. You have to have gone to the right school, with the connected coach, just to get on the radar. Everybody was just trying to convince someone to give them a shot.

After seeing my tape, UTEP called and invited me to visit. I drove out there and headed straight to an empty Sun Bowl. I walked out to midfield and just stood there, imagining sixty thousand fans looking down on me, screaming their asses off. *Dude, this is it*, I told myself.

I nailed my interviews with the coaches. They saw my passion and commitment and offered me a spot. I accepted. What do you know? Positivity had worked. All that self-talk, all those "I am Division One!" reps in the gym . . . I'd believed it, and I'd made it so. Now there was just one minor thing left to do: learn how to snap a freakin' football.

CHAPTER SEVEN

Forgiveness

Anger makes you smaller, while forgiveness forces you to grow beyond what you are.

—Chérie Carter-Scott

At one of my earliest UTEP practices, I was on the sidelines, snapping the ball over and over again. That's pretty much what I'd done all summer: clocking my way to those ten thousand hours of work that ultimately result in mastery. One of our special-teams coaches came walking over with a sour look on his face.

"Dorenbos," he said. "We were hoping for more out of you."

I got up real close, gritted my teeth, and spoke from the heart. "Don't worry, Coach," I said. "I'm a gamer. I'm like a light switch. I just turn it on."

He nodded his head slowly, with a slight smile, before moving on. Did he know, or sense, that I was full of crap? But that's just the thing: I wasn't. I guess the secret to pulling off a caper like I did is actually believing it yourself, and I would have passed a polygraph at that moment: I *was* a game-time player, and I *would* be ready.

Sure enough, from the moment I joined my teammates running out onto the Sun Bowl Stadium field in front of 31,483 screaming fans in our home opener, a 37–20 win over Southern Methodist

University, I lived up to my own hype. We had a first-year coach, Gary Nord, who had been an assistant under legendary coach Howard Schnellenberger at Oklahoma University. No one was expecting us to do anything in the Western Athletic Conference, but we ended up with a 7–1 conference record, good enough to share the league title with Texas Christian University. We played major programs like Oklahoma and Texas A&M in sold-out stadiums—*rock-star, baby!*—and we went to the 2000 Humanitarian Bowl, where we lost to Boise State.

I snapped, played some linebacker and fullback, and started to learn what it meant to be a leader in the locker room. It wasn't about giving rah-rah speeches or calling guys out; that's what the coaches were for.

A football locker room is as diverse a setting as you're going to find. We had good ol' boys from the heart of Texas, inner-city African Americans from the mean streets of St. Louis, and sons of Bible Belt preachers. Sure, we all shared in the pursuit of winning on the field, but locker room cohesion, I found, also needs guys like me: loud, positive, funny characters who could create moments that turn into memories.

I had an ability to get along with people. Remember, I had been bullied as a chubby kid, and that conditioned me to always treat everyone I came across with respect. If you were different from me, I was going to make the effort to reach out to you, to put you at ease. In a football locker room, with all those stoic tough guys, someone needs to fill that role. Team chemistry is a real thing— and thanks to my magic and the fact that you just can't stop me from cracking jokes, I realized that part of my role was keeping our team together.

For me, being positive was not only becoming a way of life but also a philosophy to believe in. When I believed my own hype about being a long snapper and then willed it to become reality, it was proof of the power of positive thinking. And when teammates crowded around my locker, craning their no-necks trying to figure out where the hell that card had disappeared to, it underscored a related truth: people want to be around positive, upbeat people.

Now, don't get me wrong, a meathead long snapper with a deck of cards didn't make all this stuff up. Ever since Norman Vincent Peale's bestselling self-help book *The Power of Positive Thinking* more than sixty years ago, millions have used techniques like visualization and daily affirmations to achieve their goals in life. In more recent times, psychologist Martin Seligman turned positive thinking into a science. Now there are reams of studies showing that negative thoughts and emotions limit the brain's ability to consider possibility; they literally result in small-mindedness. Positive thoughts and emotions—joy, love, laughter—*expand* the mind's sense of the possible.

I knew none of this back when I was sprinting like a madman down a college football field. But I was living it. Which isn't to say that I always practiced what I'm now preaching. I've always been outgoing, always liked to make others laugh and smile, but as my time at UTEP went on, I started to become aware of a vague, nagging feeling following me around.

On the field, I was killing it. During my three seasons at UTEP, I averaged ten punt-coverage tackles a year. One in particular has stayed with me to this day, 'cause it was just so cool.

We were playing an away game when my eye caught sight of the end-zone referee. Normally, you're so focused on the field that those guys aren't really people to you, they're just zebras running around. But for some reason, I saw this guy . . . and did a double take. *Holy crap, it's Mr. Wucetich*, my high school AP European history teacher. He moonlighted as a college official, and now here he was.

From the sideline, I kept my eye on him as it all came flooding back. Mr. Wucetich was one of the best teachers I'd ever had. His passion was contagious. I had no business being in an advanced placement class—I just wasn't interested in European history. I think I answered one question correctly the whole semester. It happened when he asked if anyone had ever heard of Fred Astaire and Ginger Rogers. My hand shot up, shocking Wucetich. "They were dancers, back in the day," I said.

"How do *you* know that?" he asked.

Of course, I knew about them from hearing David Copperfield reference them. "They sang and danced to this song, 'Pick Yourself Up,'" I said, "which goes, *'When my chin is on the ground / I pick myself up / Dust myself off / And start all over again.'*"

Wucetich looked like I'd just hit him with a right cross. Dorenbos talking dancing and quoting a swing tune? After all, I was the jock in the back of the class who was way more interested in the deck of cards I kept pulling out of my pocket than I was in hearing more stories about some little dude named Napoleon. Wucetich kept reminding me that there could be more for me than what I was projecting. He'd seen too many high school jocks who seemed right out of a Springsteen song sadly obsessing years later on their glory days, and he wasn't shy about pushing me to think beyond that tired story for myself.

"Mr. Dorenbos," he once said in front of the whole class, "I hope you don't become a parking lot loiterer."

"A parking lot loiterer? What's that, sir?" I asked.

"You're a Cravinite," he said, a reference to our football coach, Bill Cravin. "All you football players are Cravinites. If you let that go to your head, you're not going to do anything with your life. But you have a choice. You can be a parking lot loiterer, or you can be a beacon of the night. Be a beacon of the night, son."

I still had no idea what the hell a parking lot loiterer was, but I could tell I didn't want to be one.

Now here we were, some four years later, and we were on the

same college football field. Late in the game, we punted the ball away. I got a good jump on coverage after my snap, and I found myself bearing down on the returner deep in his own territory, about fifteen yards in front of ol' Mr. Wucetich. I approached at full speed from an angle; the ball carrier never saw me. I threw myself into him, leading with my chest. We were two locomotives colliding at top speed; the crackle of impact rocked the stadium. I heard fans gasp and I felt my rib crack. The runner was flat underneath me and wasn't moving. I jumped up and stood over him and turned to the end zone.

"*Wucetich!*" I roared. He looked at me, unsure.

"*I will get up, I will dust myself off, and I'll do this all over again, sir!*" I called out. "*Because I'm a beacon of the night!*"

I walked away, holding my rib in place. "Oh, and thanks for that D-plus," I called out over my shoulder.

Plays like that one notwithstanding, we struggled on the field my junior and senior seasons, with a combined record of four wins and nineteen losses. My senior year, I suffered a high ankle sprain, and then a hernia. When the docs gave me a shot of cortisone in the tendon of my groin, they had to be careful not to rupture the bowel line. That didn't sound like fun.

I was in a lot of pain but didn't miss a down. I'd tape up that ankle or get that injection and burst out that locker room door onto the field. Off the field, I was still the life of the party, still the guy keeping the locker room in stitches and together, which is no small feat when your team is getting its ass handed to it just about every Saturday.

But . . . something was wrong. It wasn't a thought so much as a feeling. Maybe it was related to the fact that we weren't winning or that I was pretty banged up every day. But I think it was more spiritual than that. There wasn't any one thing wrong that I could put my finger on; it felt like I was struggling to get in touch with myself, like there was an emptiness inside. Making a big tackle or entertaining a group of friends with my magic would quiet it, but the feeling kept returning. Therapy taught me to interrogate myself: *What's this about?*

I didn't know the answer, but one day, back home for a visit, I was drawn to the sands of Huntington Beach. I found myself sitting cross-legged in the exact spot I'd often return to in the years after Mom's death. It was this very spot where, when I was fifteen, I'd gone into the ocean and realized that the St. Christopher's medal Mom had left for me had snapped off the chain around my neck. My piece of her gone, I'd taken to telling myself a comforting story about this particular loss: "What a life that St. Chris medal is having," I'd tell myself—aloud— in this very spot, gazing out at the rays bouncing off the Pacific Ocean waves. "It's swimming with dolphins and catching rides with humpback whales. Pretty cool." It was one of the first times I consciously told myself a story that turned a negative into a positive.

Ever since, this was our spot, me and Mom. I'd often come to it, right at the base of the lifeguard stand, to hear myself talk to her. Sometimes I'd update her on my life: What girl I was hanging with, how the season was going. Other times, I'd tell her what Krissy was up to, or I'd relay some funny story about Susan. Now, having been led to our spot by that vaguely unsettled feeling, I found that the words just started to come, as if on their very own, and it was some *real* talk.

"You know what?" I said. "I want more in this life. I don't want to be somebody who lives in circumstance. I want to be a person of vision."

And what's been keeping me from becoming a person of vision? Sitting there, I instantly knew the answer. Suddenly, mysteriously, I was able to identify the cloud that had been hanging over me.

For years, I'd told people that I'd forgiven my dad. But had I? And, if not, why not?

"Mom," I said, my throat catching and burning, "don't get mad."

I remember looking up and realizing that part of what I was feeling was . . . *guilt.* To become that person of vision meant that I'd have to forgive my dad. *Really* forgive him. And what I was wrestling with—that cloud—was really fear. Fear that forgiving him meant I was being disloyal to Mom.

"Mom, don't get mad," I repeated, tears starting to stream. "I'm not picking sides. I swear I'm not. I'm not forgiving Dad for taking you away from us. I'm forgiving him for being lost and for making a mistake. Because I, too, have been lost and made mistakes. I'm forgiving him because I don't want him to affect my life going forward. He's not in my life anymore. You still are. And you're going to be in my life forever."

I looked around. Someone was walking a dog. A couple of dudes tossed a Frisbee around. Man, I'd been bearing all this weight, and I hadn't even been aware of it. *No one gives a shit*, I realized. "Let me get rid of carrying all this around with me," I said—pleading. "I just want to keep the goodness of you. If it were me in heaven, looking down on my son, I'd be like, 'Hell, yeah, rock on, bro. Do what you gotta do.' If I want to be the man I think you'd want me to be, I gotta ditch this cloud that's always following me around."

I sat there a good while, feeling close to Mom. Finally, I stood, took a deep breath, turned, and began making my way back to my truck in a nearby parking lot. As I walked, I could feel myself actually getting stronger. I noticed a bounce in my step. I literally felt lighter. I broke into a smile when it dawned on me: Mom pulled me here. She wanted to kick me in the ass a little: *Dude, there's something weighing on you. Just let it go, man.*

I didn't know then just how transformative real forgiveness is. "The weak can never forgive," Gandhi said. "Forgiveness is the attribute of the strong." Today, I can't tell you how many people tell me they can't forgive someone who has wronged them. I tell them to stop keeping score, man. Forgiving someone doesn't mean they win. To the contrary: letting go of bitterness and guilt frees *you*. Do it for yourself.

That's what I learned that day on the beach. Gandhi had it so right. By the time I got to my truck, I felt . . . *stronger*. I swear the cloud had lifted. I felt like I'd just grown up a little. As I began driving, I talked to Mom again. "I'm going to be okay, Mom," I said. "Whatever happens, I know now I can figure shit out. I'm always going to be able to figure shit out."

CHAPTER EIGHT

The Not For Long League

Only as high as I reach can I grow
Only as far as I seek can I go
Only as deep as I look can I see
Only as much as I dream can I be.
                              —Karen Raven

Here we go again. Setback, meet Dorenbos.

It was the night of the 2002 NFL Draft, and I'd expected to be drafted. After all, I'd wowed the pro scouts at UTEP's Pro Day combine just a month earlier. That's when a group of pro scouts visit a college team and puts its seniors through a series of drills.

I bench-pressed twenty reps of 225 pounds, and then lined up for the forty-yard dash. I was still hobbled with a hernia, but hell if I'd let the scouts see that. I was going to have to run my ass off through the pain. I'd have all summer—and maybe the rest of my life—to recover. *Moments of pain for a lifetime of glory*, I said to myself.

That's when luck—or was it Mom?—intervened. "Dorenbos, you're not really fast, are you?" barked the scout in charge.

"Uh, no, sir," I said.

"Awright, go over to the sideline," he said. "You get ten snaps."

Next to me, my teammate Sherman Austin, a blur of a tailback in a onesie speed-demon leotard, knowing I couldn't run worth a lick, muttered under his breath: "You lucky son of a bitch."

I knew what ten snaps meant: That's all I'd get, so they all had to be money. I've never been a warm-up guy, so I threw a couple of passes just to open my shoulders. "Let's do this," I said. And I bent over and snapped ten of the most picture-perfect snaps I've ever snapped.

In the NFL, a snapper who can consistently get the ball to the punter between 0.70 and 0.75 seconds is considered elite. Well, my ten snaps that day averaged 0.62 seconds; one snap was timed at 0.59. After Pro Day, Bobby April, the St. Louis Rams special-teams coach, was quoted in the newspaper as saying, "Dorenbos is the best I've seen all year, and he might be the best in a lot of years, maybe among the top guys I've ever seen."

Suddenly I was a hot property. My teammate Brian Natkin, who had an agent and who'd go on to play tight end for the Tennessee Titans, pulled me aside.

"Bro, you can play in the league," he said. He'd gone through a grueling process interviewing agents before he finally signed with one. "I got you."

Brian hooked me up with his agent, Ken Harris, who arranged interviews for me with six NFL teams. One of them, the Houston Texans, said they'd be drafting me in the fifth round.

On draft night, my roomie, Robert Clayton, and I were watching in our apartment, waiting for my name to be called. And waiting. And waiting. Sure enough, it never happened. I was pretty down—I'm not going to lie. I'd worked so hard. It was only natural to think back on all the hours in the weight room, all those snaps on the practice field, all that time spent visualizing, and to feel like it was all for nothing. But when I actually started thinking back on all those hours, the damnedest thing happened . . . the memories brought a smile to my face. Every day, I'd hit the gym with my buddies Barry and Bobby King. We'd laugh, because there was always the same body builder there, pumping weight in a cloud of chalk, as body builders do. Without fail, he'd approach me.

"Jon, would you like some chalk?"

"No, I'm cool, thanks," I'd say.

Ten minutes later: "If you need chalk just let me know," he'd call out. "The chalk's right over here."

Ten minutes after that: "I saw you looking over, Jon," he'd say. "Want some chalk?"

Every day was a chalk-centric *Groundhog Day* with my man, to the point that "Jon, do you want some chalk" became a catchphrase between me and a bunch of my buddies. I actually started chuckling to myself. See what happened? I went from feeling sorry for myself to thinking about the fun I'd had preparing for the draft—and realized that the fun was worth it, regardless of outcome.

And that led me to think of the actual work: all those reps at the gym when I'd loudly grunt, "I am *the* NFL!" If there's one thing I know, it's that you can only control what you can control. And I took care of what I could control: I put in the work. And that—the work—was a worthy end in itself.

In real time that night, I practiced resilience. I kept repeating my gym mantra back to myself—I *am* the NFL—and I bounced back. What, I'm going to let a phone that doesn't ring tell me something about who I am? Screw that noise. I went to bed that night not sure what the future held, but upbeat about its possibilities. And wouldn't you know it, as if disappointment is just another word for new opportunity, the next day Ken Harris got two phone calls, one from the Green Bay Packers, the other from the Buffalo Bills. The Bills were offering a lot less money, but I'd be the only snapper in camp. It would be my job to lose.

By day's end, I was signed as an undrafted free agent. My signing bonus? A cool $3,000. *Liv-in' large*. Once Ken had the money wired to me—it was about $1,700 after taxes—I gathered up my boys and we headed over to Stampede, the El Paso bar that was our hangout. I slammed a grand down and said to the barkeep, "My friends drink free tonight." And we got hammered. I'd made it to the Show.

A half hour after touching down for the first time at Buffalo Niagara International Airport, and just minutes after checking in at my hotel, my phone rang.

"Jon, this is Jim Kelly," said the voice on the other end. As in, Hall of Fame quarterback Jim Kelly. Calling *me*. "Listen, you're the magic guy. I'm having my charity event tomorrow—think you can perform?"

Uh, yeah, I think I can squeeze that into my schedule. I went across the street to Kmart and bought a really ugly shirt and pants. The next morning, a limo pulled up for me. When I opened the door, Kelly was inside. And . . . so was . . . then current Bills quarterback Drew Bledsoe. And . . . Dan Marino. And . . . *Jon Dorenbos*? Which one of these things doesn't belong? It was my first day in the NFL, and I found myself behind the VIP velvet rope.

The Bills head coach was Gregg Williams. He's a funny, superintense, longtime defensive coordinator—you might have seen him last year on HBO's *Hard Knocks* series inside the Cleveland Browns—and I felt from the moment the Bills signed me that he was on my side. "We're taking a chance on Jon because he's been through so much in life," he told the press at the start of the 2003 season. "I'm not really worried about his head if he has a bad snap."

The next day, Danny Smith, our special-teams coach, had something to add to Williams's public praise of me, cracking up the guys in the locker room, who I'd already taken to entertaining with my fifty-two buddies: "I'll tell you what, magic man," he said. "Too many bad snaps and I'm going to make like David Copperfield and make you disappear."

It felt like Williams and Smith were always pulling for me. Here I was, a lowly rookie long snapper, and they'd spend extra time with me, before and after practice. I gotta tell you: I wasn't very good. My snaps on field goals were fluttering ducks; later in the season, offensive lineman Trey Teague replaced me on field-goal snaps. I had trouble adjusting to the sheer speed of the game. Instead of feeling overwhelmed, or not up to the challenge, I responded to the attention from my coaches by becoming more ferocious to succeed. I'd get to practice early and stay late; I was determined to bleed for them. They bought themselves a magician when they showed faith in me.

As focused as I was, there were times when I couldn't quite believe where I was—which I recognized as a dangerous thought. My locker was between London Fletcher and Bledsoe. Fletcher was an All-Pro linebacker who would go on to start 215 consecutive games over a fifteen-year career. He was an animal who brought it every day. Bledsoe was the starting quarterback who had once led the New England Patriots to the Super Bowl, but who had gotten injured and lost his starting job to an obscure backup named Tom Brady.

Bledsoe and I had a connection, and we remain tight to this day. He sought me out on my first day. "Hey, you're the magic man," he said, putting his arm around me. "Listen, I was at Washington State when your dad's trial was in the news. I'm glad you made it, kid. You need anything, I got you."

Later—when I'd become the older dude in the locker room—

I'd always remember how much Drew's words had meant to me. Putting your arm around someone who doesn't quite fit in yet and letting them know you're pulling for them? Man, it's easy to underestimate what kind of difference that can make.

Of course, back then it was hard to convince myself I belonged in that locker room, but if you say that to yourself—*What the hell am I doing here?*—it becomes a self-fulfilling prophecy. The quickest way to torpedo your confidence is to wonder if it's justified.

It didn't take me long to identify the thing that's most present in an NFL locker room. It isn't the stink, or the stupid jokes, or the farts, though there's a helluva lot of that. You know what it is? Insecurity. That's the *real* stench in the air. A lot of dudes are scared shitless that they don't measure up, like the star wide receiver I played with who crumbled into his locker in tears when the coach got on him in front of the team. *Dude, are you serious right now? Be a man. Stand up and be accountable.*

I saw it for nearly fifteen years, and it wasn't just players. I've seen coaches who are so afraid of getting fired they sleep in their offices, going days without seeing their families. I wanted to shout to them: *Go home and make love to your wife!*

Some of the most insecure people I've ever met are superstars. They're guys who were the best in high school, the best in college. They were high draft picks and now there are a lot of expectations. So what do they do? They decide to go read social media and the papers and turn on the news and to actually take into consideration what some dude on Twitter has to say—someone who has probably never played a sport, and wouldn't dare say to your face what he tweets. They get into a rut and can't get out of their own heads, because for the first time in their lives, someone didn't tell them they were God.

I've seen young guys come into the league and try to become what they think the NFL is. They blow all their money on card games—I'm talking about rookies making the league minimum, dropping twenty thousand, trying to keep pace with the high-paid stars of the team. (Because of my magic, every team I've been on has prohibited me from dealing in card games.) They lack a sense of self, and the first time they hit a touch of adversity, they fall apart. Yes, the league's depression and suicide rates are primarily related to CTE and concussions, but don't forget the fact that in every locker room, there are widespread identity crises. There are guys who don't know who they are without football.

That's what Coach Williams was getting at when he said I'd never crumble over a botched snap. I already knew who I was. I'd already been tested. My presence in an NFL locker room was a testament to faith, a monument to the power of positive thinking, and a reminder that true mental toughness is often harder to come by than a killer time in a forty-yard dash. *You're probably faster and stronger and quicker and more experienced than me*, I thought every time I lined up across the line of scrimmage from some big guy who wanted to tear my head off. *But you're gonna have to call the cops to get me out of your face.*

See, what Coach Williams knew was that long snapper is one of those positions that tests mental skills more than physical ones. Like relief pitcher in baseball or goalie in hockey, the key to success is not letting yourself get screwed up mentally. You've got to sit for eight minutes and think about the snap that just got away from you. But your teammates just might need you to be perfect at the end of those minutes—so you'd better find a way to get to some closure. And who better than me to get to closure?

Look, let's agree that bending over and snapping a ball through your legs to another dude ain't exactly up there in terms of sacrifice and commitment when compared to, say, serving in the armed forces. But when I would walk onto the field, I took a sniper's mentality with me. You have one shot. *Get in, get out.* As early as my rookie year, I knew that if I was conscious that I was going to have to perfectly snap two hundred times over the course of the season, I'd be screwed. You want to take pressure off yourself? Just nail this one shot.

You hear athletes all the time talking about embracing the moment. I did that, yes. But it goes deeper than the usual post-game clichés. It's not just about being in the moment; it's also about processing the moment, getting over the moment, moving on from the moment, and then appreciating the new moment that *becomes* the moment. Of course, I learned that in therapy, and it's a huge part of dealing with the pressures of the Not For Long League, where the average career span is all of three seasons.

On the field my rookie year, I was like "Wild Thing" from *Major League*, which is, of course, one of the greatest movies of all time. Remember when reliever Ricky Vaughn—Charlie Sheen in the greatest role of his lifetime—came into the game to the song "Wild Thing"? *That's* the adrenaline rush that hooked me in college. Once on the mound, Wild Thing could throw heat—but had no idea where the ball was going. That was me early in my NFL career. I could snap speed, but one day our punter, Brian Moorman, said, "Look, I've punted a long time. It's gonna be four degrees outside and catching your ball is going to sting like hell."

Huh. I didn't know how to slow down my heater—when I'd try, I'd flutter those knuckleballs back there—but, okay, challenge so noted. I didn't know it at the time, of course, but Moorman's comment set me up to exhibit what the psychologists today call a "growth mind-set." I needed to go on a journey to really master this discrete skill, just like I did years before with magic.

What I grew to love about snapping was the same thing that got me hooked on magic. It was the tediousness of doing this one thing over and over and over again, until it's perfect. Until it's part of you, embedded in your muscle memory; your consciousness is no longer even a part of the act. You're not doing it to impress anyone or entertain anyone. The mastery of the act *is* the thing itself. And, at some point, you can do it the same exact way time and again when you're under pressure and people are watching you and they're trying to catch you in a screwup.

In his book *Outliers*, Malcolm Gladwell introduces the ten-thousand-hour rule—that the key to achieving expertise is practicing the right way for ten thousand hours. As I read that book, a bolt of recognition hit me: that's what I've done with magic *and* snapping. It wasn't until I was in my seventh year in the league that I finally felt like I got it—that every snap felt exactly alike. I was just a conveyor belt. And I remember what turned it around for me: I was playing in Philadelphia and had gone to a Phillies game and, for some reason, beforehand, I zeroed in on the batting-practice pitcher. I was fascinated. No one knew who this guy was, but his whole job was to give up home runs. Which means he throws more strikes than anybody. Which means he's throwing a little slower than game-day pitchers. *That's who I want to be*, I thought. The guy who serves up a home run—every time—to the punter. That's what Moorman was trying to tell me, but it took me that long—countless hours of trial and error—to figure out how to do it.

The Bills went six-and-ten in my rookie year, and I played every game. The hardest adjustment? That freakin' weather. Remember, I'm a California dude. I'd be on the field in stormy Buffalo, where we'd play in two feet of snow and the wind would blow so hard they'd have to take down the flags because they were being whipsawed off the poles, and I'd be like, "Why are we on this field right now?"

It was brutal, but experiencing those adverse conditions helped me make it as long as I did in the NFL. If you can snap in the Northeast, you can play anywhere. I've seen snappers who have played in warm-weather cities their whole careers, who suddenly struggle when they have to perform in the frozen tundra of Green Bay.

One day in the Bills' weight room, a guy who didn't seem like one of us—a player—came up to me. "Magic man!" he said. You might call Dr. Kevin Elko a sports psychologist, or an author, or a motivational speaker. He is all that, but what he really is, is a performance consultant.

There are a lot of con-man mental coaches out there with access to NFL locker rooms, but Elko, I was soon to find out, is the real deal. He knew my story and he had a corporate speaking engagement that night. Did I want to earn a few bucks and go on first, do a little magic, and share some insights from my life?

I had performed magic and played football in public, of course, but I had never really stood before an audience and talked about my life. But I had long since gotten past being embarrassed about my story. Now I was proud of the life I'd built. *What the hell*, I thought. I'm in.

I knew how to grab a room with my magic, but when I mentioned *why* I was a magician—that it was my refuge after my dad killed my mom when I was twelve—that audience was mine, in a way I'd never felt. In twenty minutes, I joked around, wowed them with some magic, *and* bared my soul.

When Elko came onstage, I saw inspiration personified. There's a reason that he's called the "head" coach of the University of Alabama football program; Coach Nick Saban has regularly had Elko deliver key pregame speeches to his team.

Elko not only makes you look at yourself; he makes you want to be a better you. For all his degrees and books and high-profile speaking gigs, he's down-to-earth and preaches common sense. He also speaks the language of the alpha male, which gives him credibility in NFL and college-football locker rooms.

The same philosophy that has made the Tide roll has helped me face challenge after challenge. Elko gave me a language to describe a lot of what I'd already been doing. Lines like "What you think causes what you feel"; "Happiness is a choice"; "Circumstances don't determine destiny"; "It didn't happen to me, it happened for me"; "The haters are out there drinking the Hatorade, and if you let them get to you, they'll turn you into them"; and "Let go of the need to be right" all hit me like the dude was singing the soundtrack to my own life.

After the first time I opened for him, Elko put his arms on my shoulders and looked deep in my eyes. "Look, if you want to do magic, that's fine and cute," he said. "But you should be a motivational speaker. This is your calling. What you just did out there was special."

From then on, he would call and offer me gigs opening for him before large groups. And he became an important mentor. At one point, as I was thinking about getting serious about motivational speaking, a speaking agent wanted me to pay $10,000 to attend a workshop that teaches how to become a million-dollar speaker.

"Jon, let me give you some advice," Elko said when I told him about it. "Don't take advice from anyone. Just be you. You don't need that shit."

He preaches being accountable—"Get rid of excuses"—and the power of connection. Put down your cell phones, he'll tell audiences, and "be where your feet are." Saban, he says, rarely uses a phone. "He doesn't e-mail, he doesn't text, and he doesn't like to talk on the phone," he says. "But he's the best at connections of anybody I've ever seen. He connects with people. Connection is intentional."

Ah, yes, intentionality—that's an Elkoism. How you speak to

yourself—the words you choose—determine outcome. "What do you say to yourself before you snap the ball?" he asked me one day.

"Uh, I don't know," I said, thinking about it. "There are times when I'm on the sideline that I say to myself, 'Oh, shit, don't screw this up,' just before going out on the field."

"That's not good," he said. "That's negative reinforcement. If you're expressing fear or doubt, you're inviting it. Why don't you just tell yourself to fire it in there and don't be a pussy?"

OMG. This is *genius*. I had always talked to myself—now I had the best thing in the world to say. From then on, just prior to every snap I've ever snapped, that's what I've said—and it freakin' works. It's all part of creating a scenario for success. Thanks to Elko, I'd create whole story lines before big plays. I'd imagine that I'm an actor in a movie and I've got only one take because the union guys have to go home and everybody on the set is hungry and all eyes are on me and I swagger out there to *Do. My. Job.* Embracing the moment, rather than shrinking from it.

My second year in Buffalo, my head filled with Elko aphorisms, I led all players at my position in the NFL in tackles. Off the field, I was growing as well. Brian Moorman's P.U.N.T. Fund—it stands for Perseverance, Understanding, Need, and Triumph—worked with the local children's hospital. I started tagging along on visits, and learning firsthand how much of a difference giving can make for the *giver*.

One day, a terminal patient—my man couldn't have been more than eight years old—told me he wanted me to go to the Super Bowl with him. He told me he had tickets. Well, using construction paper and crayons, he'd made his own Super Bowl tickets, but he'd dated them October 18.

"The Super Bowl's in February," I corrected him.

"Not this Super Bowl," he said. See, he'd been given six months to live, and October 18 was six months and *a day* since that prognosis. Beating that prognosis was *his* championship moment. I've never given anyone a more emotional high five, and then outside in the parking lot I sobbed and gasped for breath.

Another time, I picked up a twelve-year-old terminal patient at his house. He was getting to ride with me to the game; his dad would meet him at the stadium. Well, once in the car, he was breathlessly asking questions about my ride. It wasn't like I was rocking a Porsche. But he was transfixed by my Tahoe and all he wanted to be was a Buffalo Bill.

"What's the coolest thing about being a Bill?" he asked.

I answered him honestly. I loved driving to the game, passing all the tailgating fans, seeing a dad play catch with his kid outside of the stadium. And nothing beat the feeling of pulling through the gates of the players' lot. I pulled over and got out. "You know what?" I said. "You want to be a Bill, it starts with driving to the game."

I know, I know. It probably was a bit reckless. But you should have seen his face. If you have the chance to put an expression like that on a kid's face—all wide-eyed and open and joyful—how can you not? That dude rolled up into the players' parking lot like he owned the joint. And it put a lot of bounce into my step, too. Turns out, when you do good for others, it feels pretty good for you, too.

That's a lesson I carried throughout my time in the NFL. Later, in Philly, I'd head on over to Children's Hospital just to hang with kids who could use someone to hang with. I'd bring my fifty-two bros, and they'd bring out the smiles—in the kids, yes, but also in me. "For it is in giving that we receive," said St. Francis of Assisi; every time I'd leave a hospital, I'd feel better, having made someone else feel better.

I got to be pretty good at walking into a hospital ward and figuring out how to brighten the mood. I mean, it's kinda what I do. One day at Children's Hospital in Philly, I was getting nowhere with a sixteen-year-old girl. I ran through all my card tricks, and not only couldn't I get a smile out of her, I couldn't break through at all. Nothing worked. Her body had been riddled with tumors and she'd been in the hospital for months. Her mother mentioned she was depressed because she was missing her prom.

I turned to go, along with my wingman for the day, Eagles kicker David Akers. In the hallway, I turned around and looked back at her room. There she was, standing in the doorway, watching us. She was frail, and she started walking toward us, slowly sliding her feet in blue hospital socks across the floor. She shuffled up to me and hoarsely whispered, "Thank you," in my ear.

"I've got an idea," I said. "You missed your prom, didn't you? You and I can have prom right here. Let's dance."

I held out my arms, and then she was in them. Right there in the hallway. Her head rested on my shoulder as we swayed. When we parted and she made her way back to her room, her mother, tearing up, ran me down at the nurses' station. She hugged me and said her daughter hadn't spoken in months and had shown little sign of life of late. David looked at me as we walked away and said, "Man, that was magic, buddy."

"*Life* is magic," I replied.

Another time, my buddy Tim Mooney and I visited a die-hard Eagles fan who suffered from Huntington's disease, a terrible inherited disorder that results in the death of brain cells. There's no cure; patients decline into dementia and, ultimately, die. The disease had already taken two of my man's siblings *and* his daughter. Man, that was tough. As we left there, Mooney said, "If I ever complain about anything in my life, kick me in the balls."

Ultimately, that super fan passed away. His widow wanted to

spread his ashes on the fifty-yard line at Lincoln Financial Field, where the Eagles play. After a game, I brought her onto the field, where she whipped out a baggie packed full of his ashes from her bra. Seriously. I thought there'd be a sprinkling of ash; instead, there were *heaps*. When we saw the giant lawn mower start to work the field in the end zone, we knew time was of the essence. Mooney and I quickly said the Lord's Prayer; "Uh, he was Jewish," she said. We all had a good laugh as we started kicking around the ashes, trying to spread them around more evenly. It felt like a scene from *Curb Your Enthusiasm*, but it was all worth it when his widow said: "This is what he would have wanted."

I felt good, having done something for somebody else. A few years ago, a Princeton University study that gauged happiness found that no matter how much more than $75,000 per year people make, they don't report any greater degree of happiness. The researchers found that low income could create stress that makes you *un*happy, but there was no corresponding uptick after $75,000 a year. Which means, of course, that *stuff* ain't the key to a happy life, though I've been in locker rooms with dudes who think it is. It sucks not to have *enough* stuff to be comfortable, but if you really want to be happy? *That* has more to do with what you give. There's research to bear this out, but I know it from experience, too. Anne Frank wrote that "no one has ever become poor by giving," but I'd take it a step further. You actually get rich by giving. Every time I leave a children's hospital, I'm a wealthy man.

In my second season in Buffalo, I tore my ACL in Week 14. At training camp the next season, the Bills waived me. That's the Not For Long League for you; "What Have You Done For Me Lately" was, like, its theme song.

Again, it was tempting to see myself as a victim. Everything had happened *to me*, instead of just, you know: *shit happens*. But by now I knew how to get myself to accept and to move on. You know how, when I was in high school, I used self-talk to cajole myself into being Division I? And how, when I was in college, I willed myself into being in the NFL? Well, in the summer of 2005, as I was rehabbing my knee, my new mantra on every rep was "I'll be the last man standing." My teammates all had goals, too, but they usually involved making the Pro Bowl, signing a big deal, or making the Super Bowl. But I thought a pretty cool goal would be to one day be the oldest guy on my team. Because that would mean that I'd been the ultimate professional, that I showed up every day on time and ready to work, and that the guy who signed my checks thought enough of me to have me around for a long time.

But now that wasn't going to happen. It didn't take me very long to accept it and move on. *That was fun*, I thought. I'd gotten to spend two years in the NFL. Now it was time to go figure out the rest of my life. Right? Well, what I didn't count on was the fact that being the oldest dude on a team didn't *have* to apply only to the Buffalo Bills.

CHAPTER NINE

We Are Family

Life is not measured by the number of breaths we take, but by the moments that take our breath away.

—George Carlin

"Bob Stull says you're my guy," said the soft-spoken bear of a man with a nervous tic of a cough. It was November of 2006. Philadelphia Eagles coach Andy Reid had been an offensive coach under Stull back in the 1980s, when Stull—now the UTEP athletic director—had coached at my alma mater. Now there were seven games left in the season and Reid's long snapper, Mike Bartrum, had broken his neck. Reid needed someone, and he needed someone fast. Stull had called to tell him he had just the guy.

By now, I was officially a journeyman NFL player. After the Bills waived me, I'd been picked up and released *twice* by the Tennessee Titans. So I'd become a veteran of the coldhearted Not For Long League. I was a hired gun, and I was okay with that. Once I'd used up my worth to a team, I'd ride off into the sunset like Clint Eastwood in *High Plains Drifter*. *That* was cool, I'd think, and head back to Cali and my magic and my friends.

Now Reid stood before me, just before my Eagles tryout. He didn't move his head, but looked me up and down with his eyes.

There was a faint smile—at least I think there was, because it was always hard to tell with his big, bushy mustache—and he turned and walked away.

Out on the field, there were three of us who had been called in. One was Jon Condo, a talented snapper who would go on to play for the Raiders for a dozen years. The other candidate was Adam Johnson, a young dude who I'd mentored when I was with the Bills and he played for the University of Buffalo. Great kid, but c'mon: I can't lose out to someone I was coaching just a couple of years ago, right?

Eagles punter and field-goal holder Dirk Johnson was on the field to receive our snaps, crouched down on one knee eight yards away, his hand outstretched, ready to catch each snap before holding it down for an imaginary kicker. Each of us would get ten chances. It was do-or-die. Each snap needed to be about fifty miles per hour, precisely three and a half rotations in a tight-ass spiral, the ball arriving into Dirk's hands laces up and outward. If one snap went even slightly awry . . . you're off the island, my man.

"Fire in it there, don't be a pussy," I said aloud before each one. And they were money. But so were Condo's and Johnson's. After, the three of us were headed back to the locker room when special-teams coach John Harbaugh yelled out, "Hey, Jon, hang back." Soon Coach Reid emerged from the tunnel, with that slight, sideways smile.

"You *are* my guy," he said. "Listen, I don't care what you do. You want to go home? Go home. You want to snap? Snap. You want to lift weights? Lift. You want to run? Run. I don't care. But if that snap ain't there on Sunday, you're fired. Clear?"

Whoa. "Yessir," I said.

"See you at practice," Coach Reid—who will forever be Big Red to me—said, turning and walking away. From that moment on, Big Red had purchased himself the loyalty of a long snapper.

If there's one thing I hate, it's being babied. I had to grow up real fast as a twelve-year-old, and ever since, I've taken it as a slap in the face when a coach—or any authority figure—treated me like anything other than a man. When I left the state of Washington and finished my therapy, I vowed that I'd never be babysat. Coaches who check on players for curfew drove me nuts—not because I wanted to go out partying, but because it made me feel infantilized. Now here was a coach talking to me like I was a man: I don't care *how* you get the job done. Just get it done.

From that day on, Big Red was someone I wanted to make proud. Someone I would run through brick walls for. And I wasn't the only one. A locker room full of men, I'd soon learn, would take to the field and play their butts off each week for the big guy on the sidelines. I've had great coaches, but none inspired the kind of loyalty in so many players like ol' Big Red did.

Reid's Eagles had been to the Super Bowl two years earlier, losing to the Patriots, and they were still—and would continue to be—among the league's elite. By the time I joined the team around midseason, our star quarterback, Donovan McNabb, had been lost to a season-ending injury. We were five and six when backup quarterback Jeff Garcia showed me how much leadership means to a team.

In his book *The Captain Class: The Hidden Force That Creates the World's Greatest Teams*, author Sam Walker says there are great players, yes, but that most great teams are not made by them or, for that matter, by great coaches. Walker's exhaustive study found that it's usually one great leader who turns a team from good to great—and it's almost never the most talented player. Michael Jordan was, by far, the best player on his dominant Chicago Bulls teams in the nineties. But, Walker argues, the doggedness and humility of seven-foot center Bill Cartwright was as crucial in leading that team to victory as were Jordan's dunks.

On our team, Donovan McNabb was immensely talented, and a good teammate, but you wouldn't exactly call him an inspirational leader. When he went down with that knee injury in 2006, the media wrote the team off. But they underestimated a locker room full of men, not least of whom was our backup quarterback.

Garcia wasn't a big, imposing guy, but he had the heart of a mountain lion, and that competitive spirit caught on. He'd been a Pro Bowl quarterback a few years before with the San Francisco 49ers, so he had skill, but it was his ability to rally guys around him that made all the difference. It wasn't that he was a loud, rah-rah kind of guy. That's acting, not leadership. No, Jeff Garcia showed up every day to do the work—first one to practice, first one out of the tunnel—and in the way he carried himself he demanded that you do the same. He wasn't out late, going to strip clubs, talking shit. A leader is not someone who points fingers and yells and screams. A leader is someone who people follow because, in everything he does, he puts others first.

When I first got to Philly, it struck me that everyone in our locker room believed in their bones that we were going to win. I've been on talented teams—my second year in Buffalo comes to mind—where you could just tell that some guys on either side of you had checked out. They stopped believing.

In Philly, we went on a run behind Jeff because of the confidence he gave off. If we were losing, it didn't matter. We'd look at him, take in his body language and his positivity, and even if he didn't say anything, you just felt: *We're good. We're gonna figure this out.* Over eight games that season, Jeff threw ten touchdowns against only two interceptions, we won five straight and the NFC East Division, and he made the cover of *Sports Illustrated.* And *then* he led us to a playoff win over the New York Giants.

Some guys just make others believe, and for nearly the next decade, the Eagles had many of those players. Throughout the league,

The happy family on vacation. When Dad killed Mom
five years later, the violence came out of nowhere.

Whether we were fishing together or playing catch
in the front yard every night, Dad was my hero.

All Mom ever wanted was to be a mom. And she was great at it.
I had her for only twelve years, but I talk to her every day.

July 4, 1993: nearly a year after Mom died, Krissy and I went to live
with Aunt Susan in Southern California. *Left to right*:
Krissy, Susan, and me.

The first time I fell in love. That's Michael Grove,
showing me up-close magic. I was hooked.

After Mom died, magic saved me. Ken Sands, who owns
an Orange County magic store, was my first coach. I'd call him
twenty times a day.

All I wanted to do after Dad killed Mom was make the Dorenbos name stand for something positive and make my grandparents, Poppy and Nonnie, proud.

I followed my high school and junior college buddy Paul Tessier to the University of Texas at El Paso, where we played at Sun Bowl Stadium before packed houses. It was totally rock-star.

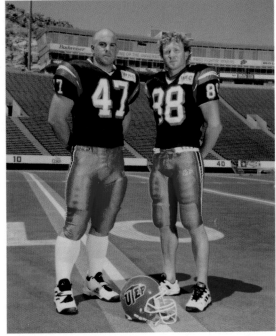

My first day in the NFL: at Bills legend Jim Kelly's charity event, hanging with (*left to right*) actor Chris McDonald and NFL stars Dan Marino and Jason Taylor. I'm like: Are you kiddin' me?

They said I'd be out six to eight weeks with torn ligaments in
my ankle. Screw that noise. I made this solo tackle instead—
my favorite play.

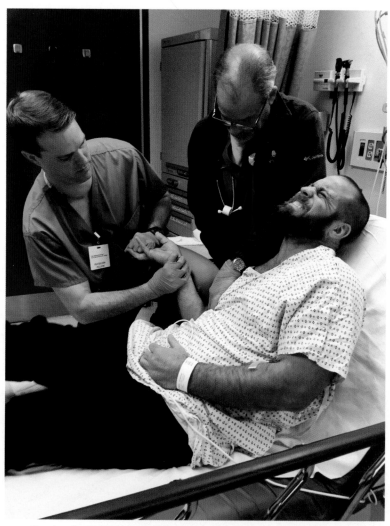

On the day I tied the Eagles' team record for consecutive games played—162—I dislocated my wrist. You want to talk pain? Three surgeries later, I was on my way back.

Our first date. By the end of it, Annalise was moving in with me.
She turned my heart right side up.

Among my influences as a performer is Iron Mike Tyson,
who, in his one-man show, isn't afraid to bare his soul.

The best day of my life. That's my man Tim Mooney—
who introduced us—officiating at our wedding.

Ellen and I clicked right away. She is what you see on TV: relentlessly positive, joyful, and fully in every moment.

With *America's Got Talent* judges Howie Mandel and Simon Cowell. Though I didn't win in the finals, what a great ride!

During my month-long recovery from emergency open-heart surgery, Annalise and I would walk the hospital floor each day, raising spirits—including our own.

I never wanted a dog. But, drugged up and recovering from heart surgery, I fell in love with this guy, Saint.

For me, performing magic has never been about the trick. It's been about the adrenaline rush of connecting with an audience and making their day better.

After twenty-six years, I had lunch with my dad.
"I forgive you for being lost," I told him.

Family. Love. Safety.

there are players (not to mention coaches and executives, for that matter) who don't want to win so much as be the *reason* their team wins. Ego kills, man. You get one guy who places himself above the brotherhood and the whole vibe can collapse. But you get a bunch of guys who place "we" over "me" in everything they do? Man, you're gonna win some football games.

For example, you couldn't be around safety Brian Dawkins— and his alter ego, Weapon X—and *not* try your damnedest to find a gear you never knew you had. Dawkins was so intense, so driven, so focused . . . it made you realize you could *always* do more.

And then there was my man Jon Runyan. Jon was an All-Pro left tackle for fourteen years. A poll of NFL players in 2008 found that being blocked by the six-foot seven-inch, 330-pound Runyan on a screen pass was one of the scariest things in the league. After he retired, Jon went on to become a US congressman and now works for the NFL. But to me, Jonny Runyan will always be a guy who made everyone around him better.

Big Jon didn't have to say a word in the locker room. He led in his very being. Think about this. Big Jon played for months with a broken tailbone. He had to ride everywhere in a sprinter bus with a pole in the center of it, because he couldn't sit down. We played at San Francisco and he stood on the long plane ride there and back after playing an NFL game.

"How are you doing this, dude?" I said to him. "How are you playing everyday when you can't even sit down?"

"Oh, that's easy," he said. "Just don't fall down."

That's why I loved Jonny Runyan: *Just don't fall down.* Easy.

Like most long snappers, I'd long been a mercenary. But then, in Philly, the damnedest thing happened. I'd found security in the Eagles family, and in the city as a whole. Generally, long snappers toil in anonymity. No one knows what we do, let alone who we are. But in Philly, the most sports-crazed of towns, something happened. Shortly after I arrived, a local reporter, Joe Santoliquito, approached me and commented on how serendipitous it was that the song "Wind Beneath My Wings" was sung at my mom's funeral—with its line about flying higher than an eagle—and here I was, *playing* for the Eagles. Whoa. "You're going to do great things here," that writer said, and his words became a type of self-fulfilling prophecy. Not only did that Bette Midler song instantly become the pregame soundtrack in my headphones—while my teammates psyched themselves to rap backbeats or ear-splitting heavy metal, but the city and I just clicked, like it was destiny. People started recognizing me. Out to dinner, I'd get high fives. At the supermarket, a fan might yell "Magic man!" and ask for an autograph.

The Eagles asked me to host a weekly TV show during the season. I'd interview my teammates, make them the victim of my card tricks. How sick is this: in 2009, I won an Emmy, for best host. Suddenly I started seeing fans wearing Eagles number 46 jerseys. With my name on the back. What the . . . ? I'd go up to strangers on the street who were wearing my jersey and offer to sign it for them. "You do know I'm just a long snapper, right?" I'd say to them.

People sensed that I was more than a hired gun. I was an Eagle. I was a Philadelphian. My family had shattered when I was twelve, and without really planning it, my team and this amazing city had become my extended family. Before, snapping a football was a job. Now, quite by accident, I'd found a higher purpose. When our team owner, Jeffrey Lurie, got married, I was the only player invited to the wedding. "You're family," he said, and I beamed inside.

It wasn't unrelated that my play improved year after year. After all, wouldn't you go all out for *your* family? In 2010, I made the Pro Bowl, and would again five years later. Ever since 1979, when the disco song "We Are Family" was the theme song for the World Series champion Pittsburgh Pirates, sports-team marketing departments have painted their franchises as families. But for me, the idea of the Eagles as family wasn't just some sports-page cliché. For me, it meant bringing to our relationship the same type of commitment we all bring to our actual families.

One day, for example, the team doc brought some grave news. I had torn ligaments in my ankle. Out six to eight weeks, at least. Big Red came to see me. "I'm not going to put you on injured reserve," he said. "If we make the playoffs, I want you there."

If Andy put me on injured reserve, I'd miss the rest of the season. Instead, he was going to keep me on the active, fifty-three-man roster. Which meant I was taking up a roster spot. Which meant someone was getting fired so they could clear a spot for a temporary snapper to come in.

Well, that didn't sit right. Not if we were *really* family. If we're really a band of brothers, I couldn't let one of my mates go down because of me. The clincher for me was when I read a quote from my teammate Brian Dawkins in the paper. "I play the game the way a fan would play if he had a chance to strap on a uniform for one game," he said.

Man, that sealed it. If you went to a die-hard, face-painted Eagles fan and said, "You can play in one game, but you're going to have to play through the pain of torn ligaments in your ankle, would you do it?" *None* of them would think twice. Before you finished asking the question, they'd be at the stadium, getting padded up.

Screw it, I thought. I had a week to get ready. "Let's rehab this," I said to our trainer, Rick Burkholder, who nodded his head and said, "Fuck, yeah." Rick was up for the challenge.

I moved into the training facility and rehabbed around the clock. Three hours on, two hours off, three hours on, two hours off. The pain was excruciating. I just kept telling myself that old adage again: *Moments of pain for a lifetime of glory.*

By Friday, if I really concentrated, I could hide my limp and jog slowly in a straight line. Big Red came into the trainer's room. "What's it gonna be, kid?"

"I'll be there for you on Sunday, Coach," I said.

There was that sideways smile again. "Good to see you still have a little linebacker left in you," he said.

Come game day, I took a couple of shots to numb the area. It was totally legal. And it was what I had to do. I'd been listed as "questionable," so when the team was out on the field for the pre-game warm-up, the Giants had their special-teams coach, Tom Quinn, keeping his eye on me. If I was seen limping or in pain, they could keep me off the field, or worse, they could go right for my injury, seeking to knock me out of the game. Man, it was painful pretending I wasn't in pain. I just grunted my way through every step. Just before kickoff, one of our assistant coaches, David Culley, asked how I was doing.

"I'll tell you how I'm doing," I said. "I'm gonna make a solo tackle and I'm gonna snap a game-winning field goal to win this muthafucka."

He looked at me kinda funny. "Don't go crazy," he said. "Just snap the ball and get off the field."

Well, first snap, I made it down the center of the field untouched until . . . I was helmet to chest with the ball carrier. *Boom.* Check solo tackle off today's to-do list. Then, with less than two minutes remaining, I snapped the ball on what turned out to be the game-winning field goal. Talk about positive thinking and visualization.

Afterward, in the training room, the trainers took the tape off my ankle and it was blown up, all blue and black and purple. We were icing it when Big Red walked in. He'd always carry a pen that he'd click over and over again. He stopped, looked at me, clicked his pen twice, and gave me a nod.

That nod meant the world to me. It's the nod football coaches like Andy Reid give when they know you've played through an injury that should have kept you off the field. It's a nod that says, *I understand you did a hard thing. I respect the doing of hard things.*

That nod spoke volumes. Later, at my locker, a couple of guys walked by, also pausing to give me a nod. They were the ones who were on the bubble, and they knew it. Had I not gutted it out, one of them would have been fired. That's what you do in a family: You place the others in it before you. And it starts at the top.

The thing players loved about Andy was the same thing the media hated about him: he never threw anybody under the bus. If a player called an ill-advised time-out, there Big Red would be at the postgame press conference: "Yeah, that was my call," he'd say. "That was my mistake. I've got to do a better job there."

As a player in that scenario, you'd go into the locker room expecting your boneheaded play to become fodder for reams of newsprint, not to mention breathless criticism from the TV and radio talking heads. But then you'd look at your coach, that big dude with a 'stache, and you'd start to see him as a type of human bulletproof vest, taking incoming meant for you, and not even thinking twice about it. Again, family. How can you not give your all for a guy like that?

Those great Eagles teams I played for under Andy for seven seasons starting in 2006 weren't necessarily full of superstars. But we were a group of men, not boys. We were a group of men who handled ourselves like men, who treated each other like men, who loved a coach who said, "Yo, I care about you. I care about your families. I'm pulling for you and I'm here to help make you better." We proved that if you get a group of guys together sharing that kind of commitment, nobody can stop that.

At least for a while, that is. Between 2006 and 2010, our record was 48–31–1, with two division titles and four playoff appearances. By 2012, though, the results on the field were no longer there. Our longtime defensive coordinator, Jim Johnson, passed away in 2009; with Johnson running the defense, Reid had been able to concentrate on the offensive side of the ball. When I first became an Eagle, Reid and Johnson were among those crowding around me one day to see some magic tricks. I lifted Johnson's watch right off his wrist without him even knowing it—and news of that quickly made its way throughout the building. Everyone was so tickled that Johnson had been one of my good-natured victims, because he was just so beloved. After his death, something was missing. Our eight-and-eight record in 2011 dropped to four-and-twelve in 2012.

Big Red was fired at the end of that season. Sometimes, in the NFL, players need to hear a different voice—and coaches need to have a different group of listeners. That was the case here. Andy moved on to Kansas City, where all he did was win again. And our locker room was about to receive a jolt of energy when college coaching phenom Chip Kelly was hired.

CHAPTER TEN

You Can't Fake Football

Be thankful for what you have, you'll end up having more. If you concentrate on what you don't have, you will never, ever, have enough.

—Oprah Winfrey

Under Chip Kelly, the Eagles became a national story. Chip was a tsunami of energy, and he had taken Andy's four-and-twelve team and led us to a ten-and-six record in 2013. Of course, turnarounds like that happen in the NFL, where parity has become the norm. Over the course of a season, only a handful of key plays may, in the end, separate the league's elite teams from its also-rans.

The reason people were talking about us wasn't our improved record so much as *how* Chip was coaching. He was an offensive innovator, bringing with him from Oregon a dynamic RPO—run, pass, option—offense that was all about tempo. He would run more plays faster than anyone else—ever. At first, Chip's system took the NFL by surprise. (Until opposing defenses caught up, as happens.)

Chip—who I loved playing for, and who I still speak with today—was great at talking to, and inspiring, the team as a group. He became known for his focus on mental conditioning and sports science.

Chip was dead-on when he observed that NFL teams spend way too long timing how fast guys run rather than evaluating their mental toughness. I knew this firsthand. I can't tell you how many coaches over the years would shake their heads and tell me that my knee-to-ankle ratio was off, or act like they needed to time my sprints with a friggin' calendar.

None of that technical stuff measured the heart of a man, which often made the difference come Sunday. And my whole game was all about heart: *You can hit me as hard as you want and I will stand up every damn time. Because what you can do to me ain't shit compared to what I've been through. So let's go.*

So I loved it when Chip would bring in motivational speakers to help get us into top mental shape. Like the time one speaker placed a couple of two-by-four wooden beams on the locker room floor and had us all walk on them, from one end to the other. Guys were moonwalking, side-shuffling, laughing up a storm.

"Pretty easy, right?" our speaker asked. Yeah, of course.

But then our attention was called to a photo of ironworkers hard at work, walking across metal beams some two hundred feet in the air. "How easy would *that* be?"

Uh, that's kinda different. "Why? Guys, it's the same thing," our speaker said. "You guys just did it, backpedaling, laughing. If you're going to clam up at two hundred feet, what's the difference? You looked around. You let outside factors affect the task at hand."

Wow. That really spoke to me, as someone who has learned that the story we tell ourselves ultimately determines our reality. I could tell it got the other guys thinking, too. Just how much were our thoughts holding us back?

Chip liked to say, "You can't fake football," and he was so right. It's what Coach Hay was getting at back at Golden West, when he told us that our conduct on the football field would reveal our character. But beware of anyone who thinks he's discovered *the* answer; sometimes Chip's emphasis on mental conditioning and sports science could go too far.

Don't get me wrong: I loved Chip, and still do. He motivated and inspired me. And his intentions were good. But here's what I learned during that time: if you ran into someone in the facility and asked why they were there and the answer was "to support the thesis I'm writing," well, they probably should find somewhere else to hang out. The only answer should be, "I'm here to help this team win football games."

Chip *was* all about winning, and he wanted to give the players every opportunity to get an edge. But once he hired three guys as his sports-science gurus, they hooked us up to electrodes so much that players started to feel like lab rats. The days became more about a checklist of useless tests than winning football games.

In my case, they tried to tell me that some of their tests showed I must be depressed, and that I drank too much and didn't sleep enough. Puh-leeze. I love life. I rarely drink. And I sleep like a freakin' log. Then the sports-science guys and special-teams coach Dave Fipp sat me and punter Donnie Jones down and told us to write on a three-by-five card three thoughts we have before snapping and punting, respectively. Donnie and I looked at each other.

"I don't think anything," I said.

"Me too," Donnie said. "I punt the damn ball."

Asking what I think about before I snap the ball shows you lack understanding about what football is all about. It's about *not* thinking, geniuses. It's about training your muscle memory so you can shut off distracting thoughts and just focus on the task at hand. Ever since my rookie year in Buffalo, when, thanks to Elko, I started muttering "fire it in there, don't be a pussy" to myself before snapping, my life had been a testament to what the Buddhists call the state of "no mind." Now here were these sports-science guys and Coach Fipp insisting that I *was* thinking out on the field, and accusing me of not taking their questions seriously.

They put GPS trackers in our footballs and wanted to crunch the numbers with us. I told them to go have themselves a party with their charts but to leave me out of it. Not because I'm some kind of rebel, but because I know what works for me.

"I'm not curing cancer here," I told the sports-science crew. "I'm taking a ball and snapping it between my legs like an idiot. Let's just keep it that simple. When I start overcomplicating it and overthinking, I play bad."

They were insistent, though, that I really *was* thinking—and I was in denial. Well, wouldn't you know it? That refrain from them became a self-fulfilling prophecy. Against the Miami Dolphins, leaning over the ball, for the first time in years, I was aware of my own thoughts. I was *self*-conscious, when the goal is to transcend consciousness. I snapped the ball . . . and it went high and right of the punter . . . and the punt was blocked.

You succeed at sports the same way you succeed at life: By *overcoming* negative self-talk. How much was my brain shut off during games? If you asked me the score during a game and I told it to you, I was thinking way too much. There were times when I thought we were going into halftime when the game was actually over. Remember that Kevin Costner movie *For the Love of the Game*? He plays a pitcher throwing a perfect game who doesn't even realize it, because he's flashing back on his life throughout all nine innings. I recognized myself in that character—though Costner can't really pull off my leading-man chops.

Seriously, it probably would have horrified the sports-science guys to know just how out of it I was during games. One time while on the sideline, I noticed Kevin James and Vince Vaughn on the field. They were promoting their new movie, *The Dilemma*. They were at the other end zone, walking around, high-fiving fans.

I'm a big Kevin James fan. *Oh my God*, I thought. *If ever there's a time I can meet Kevin James and he'll think I'm cool, it's now, when I'm in uniform.* I started pulling for our offense to get a first down so I could still be on the sideline when he got near. As he was getting closer, I ran down the sideline to meet him, right near one of the coaches, who looked at me and said, "Where are you going?"

"Coach, it's Kevin James," I said. He just looked at me blankly—I don't think he understood. Just then, the offense came up short on third down, so I had to get on field for the punt. By the time I got back, I could see James and Vaughn walking into the tunnel. And I slammed my helmet on the ground and cursed.

"What happened?" one of the coaches asked.

"Man, Kevin James walked into the tunnel—*that's* what happened!" I snapped.

My teammates shied away from me a little after that. But there was a method to that madness. I don't overthink snapping—and asking about thinking actually *encourages* overthinking. You put in all those hours training to let your body take over—so you can be free to go stalk Kevin James on the field.

I'm a wired, high-energy guy—the frantic magician onstage is no act—but to succeed on the field I learned I had to slow down my heart rate. Before games, my teammates Connor Barwin and Jason Kelce would punch each other in the face at their lockers while Donnie Jones and I would cower, hoping they wouldn't turn their pregame rage on us. Well, that's what *they* needed. I needed just the opposite; I'd listen to "Wind Beneath My Wings"—Mom's song—and actually nap at my locker right up until it was time to take the field. Kicker David Akers would wake me and I'd run out there after a ten-minute power nap, ready to roll.

I knew from knowing myself that if my heart rate was too elevated, my snaps would be, too. They'd go high, or wobble, or just be slightly off. So I turned snapping into a magic move.

People like to say "the hand is quicker than the eye," but that's not really true. A killer move in magic doesn't come from speed, it comes from being calculated, from being trained, from slowing everything down around you. The most beautiful magic moves are the opposite of fast; they're slow and smooth. Once I had boiled my job down to its simplest parts on the football field—naturally, without thinking—I was able to perform consistently.

But now I had found myself smack-dab in the middle of a culture clash, confronted by a philosophy that, whether intended or not, complicated what I did. In recent years, sports has been overrun by nonathletic dudes in lab coats and computer geeks. I get it—they can play an important role, and coaches are wise to latch on to anything that can give them an edge. But sometimes you can have too much data, and because you've made up your mind that you've discovered *the* secret to the football universe, you can assign meaning to data that is essentially meaningless.

That's what the sports-science guys didn't get. How bad was it? They sewed GPS tracking devices into our jerseys during practice. Once, when I was leaving the practice field, one of these dudes came up to me, breathless.

"Jon, congratulations!" he said. "You hit a personal record today."

"Really? In what?" I hadn't done much. Practiced a few snaps and generally tried to look interested.

"Look at your chart," he said, shuffling through his papers. "You ran eighteen-point-nine miles per hour today."

Huh? In all the data they'd collected on me during practice, I had *never* run faster than six miles per hour. Come to think of it, I hardly ever ran at all. How could I have run so fast? Bryan Braman was the fastest special-teams player, and he consistently logged in at twenty-one, maybe twenty-two miles per hour. I'm, like two miles per hour slower than one of the fastest guys on the team? I don't think so.

I wracked my brain. *Wait a minute*, I thought. *I didn't even put my cleats on today.* But I *did* drive the cart around in practice, and probably hit 18.9 miles per hour on the straightaway heading to the practice bubble. I started cracking up. "You guys' heads are so far up your own ass your common sense is gone," I told the sports-science genius. "You timed me driving a friggin' cart!"

Don't get me wrong: I'm not *anti*-science. Global warming is real and man-made. But I am anti–*junk* science, and the more these sports-science gurus talked in acronyms to us, the more it felt like this was a fad dressed up as fact. Turns out, there were some significant red flags behind much of the sports-science research that should have led coaches to keep it all in perspective. For example, most of the studies cited—like the one that prescribed a stretch for me that didn't do jack shit—were based on a statistical method unique to sports science. It's called Magnetic Based Inference, or MBI.

It's a complicated formula, and I ain't no scientist, but an investigation by Christie Aschwanden and Mai Nguyen at FiveThirtyEight.com laid bare the fundamental problem with it. If, say, you want to determine whether a stretch can improve athletic performance, the tried-and-true method is to recruit highly fit volunteers and conduct lab tests on them over a long period of time. That takes a while and usually results in small sample sizes. MBI gets around these problems by relying on a statistical approach embedded in Excel spreadsheets, making it more speculative—a *prediction*—than a report of actual facts.

The result? As Stanford University's Kristin Sainani reported in the journal *Medicine & Science in Sports & Exercise*, MBI lowers the standard of evidence and increases false-positive rates. Now, I couldn't actually *debate* the sports-science dudes on any of this. They'd, like, use big words. But remember, I'm a guy who fudged his way into a college scholarship, and you can't BS a BSer. I sensed it was BS when they were talking to me, and now, lo and behold, come studies that show that much of it was just that.

Here's the thing. Even if all the science behind it was dead-on, the fadlike rush to embrace sports science as if it was *the* answer ignored the truth about what really makes for success in football. This I know: it's that Band of Brothers, bros-being-bros culture that my man Jon Runyan carried in his very being. I had to laugh when the science guys told us that having a few beers wiped away the benefits of two weeks of training. Well, let me tell you the football roster I want around me. I want a team of Jon Runyans. I want a guy who drinks whiskey straight and punches you square in the face, flicks his cigarette to the ground, and goes home. That's who I want—rather than the guy hooked up to wires running on a perfectly smooth track attached to a parachute.

No, give me the guy who has holes in his boots, who drives a beat-up truck, who drinks a beer in one gulp, and who, when you look at his wife the wrong way, just knocks you out and then goes back to eating a rare steak. I'll take that guy any day, because that's the game we play. That guy? When the shit hits the fan, he's going to be a little more calm, cool, and collected than the dude being timed at the $100-million training facility.

My problem wasn't with Chip; it was with the guys he brought in to run tests on us. Man, we're a roomful of alpha males. You'd better come at us with some credibility or you're gonna suffer some consequences. Once, they put me in a chair and stood around talking shit to me, to test my response: "Jon, you're a slow piece of shit, you don't run fast, I'm going to destroy you . . . "

One of these guys asked me, "What are you feeling right now, Jon?"

Seriously? What was this, psych class? I looked at him and said: "Well, I'm slow, but I'm still here, playing this game. Dude, who *are* you? Why am I even wasting my time listening to you? Like, are you serious right now? Motherfucker, I lost my family when I was twelve. You think I give a shit about what you *say* to me?"

After that Miami game in which I thought about thinking instead of just *doing*, I was done with these jokers. I had a couple of shaky games and the Eagles auditioned a couple of long snappers. The media crowded around my locker, wondering how I felt about that. Why the hell was everyone so curious about my *feelings* all of a sudden?

"Let me tell you something," I said. "If someone on the street is better than I am, that's my fault for even opening the door. They're not my competition. My competition"—and, here, I pointed to my head—"is right here."

I remember telling the reporters, "Look, I've been through a lot worse than a couple of bad snaps," and I flashed back on a slide Chip once showed the whole team. It was a photo of a tiger and the caption read: "Tigers don't lose sleep over the opinions of sheep." Hell, yes, that's me: a tiger, albeit one without a lot of, uh, foot speed. But that slide spoke to me. The opinions of people who don't matter are of no consequence to me. The worst thing a specialist in sports can do is get stuck in his own head. I politely told the sports-science guys they could kiss my ass. To go ahead with their numbers and charts and experiments, but I didn't want to hear one word about them. A lot of my teammates felt the same way. Our checklist of tests was killing team morale.

Chip spent three seasons in Philly, and our record got worse each year. We finished seven-and-nine in 2015 and he was fired. Now, don't get me wrong: I still believe Chip is an awesome coach. He was damn right that there's no faking football. Some sports, you can run around and blend in. But when we put on that game film on Mondays? It's you and the guy lined up across from you, and there's no getting around that. Coaches like to say, "There's no 'I' in *team*," but Chip would point out: "There's an 'I' in *win*."

He wanted our self-talk to be personally accountable, but for the good of the team: *I* will dominate this play, *I* will not let my team-mates down.

That's deep stuff, and it made me a better player. But for a lot of us, the emphasis on sports science under Chip not only wasn't what football was all about, it got in our heads and distracted us from what worked. After I told the sports-science guys to party on without me, I went back to thinking about precisely nothing. And in 2015, I made the Pro Bowl again.

CHAPTER ELEVEN

Salvation

Happiness can be found in the darkest of times, if only one remembers to turn on the light.

—J.K. Rowling

My friends thought Big Dom's last name was "Cool as Shit," because that's how I always referred to him: *Big Dom, who is cool as shit.* Dom DiSandro's title might have been vice president of team security for the Philadelphia Eagles, but he looked like a bouncer at a trendy club and was as down-to-earth as they come. He was one of the most popular dudes in the Eagles locker room. One day during training camp in 2014, Dom came to the locker room to get me and ushered me into his office for what I can only describe as an intervention.

There, waiting for me on the phone, was my man Elko. I'd been talking on the phone to him a lot, because I was in a bad place. Obviously, he hadn't liked what he heard. He enlisted Big Dom's help in getting me mano a mano for an hour.

What was the problem? My marriage was crumbling. Julie and I had met when she attended one of my motivational speeches, and we got married in 2010. Out of respect to her—and, really, outta respect for that nondisclosure agreement I signed to save a whole lotta money—I'm not going to go into detail about how our marriage unraveled by year five. Suffice it to say, I started to learn she wasn't who I thought she was. So there I was, talking to crowds about how happiness is a choice and about how liberating closure can be, and yet *I'd* fallen into a deep, dark hole.

I was losing weight. I was depressed. I was crying all the time. And I was angry. And when I say angry . . . I mean *angry*. My friends must have grown tired of all the expletive-laden rants I subjected them to. How angry was I? Man, I'm embarrassed to say that for the first time in my life, I had an inkling of understanding as to how my dad could have totally lost it. Deep, huh? Thankfully, because of all the therapy and self-talk, even while I was spiraling, I had the presence of mind to tell myself over and over not to be like my dad. Not to react in the moment . . . and lose everything.

Elko heard the anger and depression in my voice, and now here he was. "Jon, why are you so angry?" he asked.

"Man, I'm being put through all this shit," I vented. "I'm pissed off." Even though I'd practiced self-interrogation for the past two decades, I couldn't hear the "woe is me" victim story I was telling myself.

"Yeah, but why?" Elko probed. "I've heard you speak a ton of times and you're always talking about forgiving your dad. I've never once heard you talk shit about anybody. Why are you start-ing now? You don't let people in your past affect your future, so why are you letting that happen now?"

Elko had a way of verbally punching me in the gut. Now he'd stopped me cold. "Damn," I said. "I guess I kinda lost myself."

"It's all good, Jon," he said. "Just find yourself and move on. Don't hate, don't blame. Forgive."

In the course of an hour conversation, we talked about things I already knew but had let my pain obscure. How the downfall of man is ego, and how taking everything personally is nothing more than ego run amok. My best friend, Danny Emmons, who'd been running with me since junior high, had some wise advice. "You know what? You just have to step back and realize she's not you," he said. "And she might not think like you."

It's that prideful, egocentric part of ourselves that fights what is right in front of us, that resists closure. Expecting everyone to treat you the way you treat them is more about *you* than them.

"Your ex is not a villain, Jon," Elko said, breaking through my judgmental, egocentric self. "The bottom line is you guys have two cups and they just need to be filled differently. Let me ask you something. Did you love your wife?"

"Yeah, I adored her."

"Notice the past tense," Elko remarked. "You've since found out some things about her. Do you love *that* woman?"

"No," I said.

"So you love the image of who you *thought* she was," he said.

One of the many issues between Julie and me was my desire to fly airplanes. It satisfied my thirst for adventure *and* helped calm me. Up in the clouds, I felt closer to Mom. Julie thought I was being reckless and stupid. Now Elko brilliantly connected the conversation to that.

"That image of who you thought she was? Why don't you go find *that* person?" he said. "Jon, you're thirty-five years old, you have no kids. You thought Julie was that person who could fly through life with you. She's not. Now go find that person."

Whoa. Elko is good, man. *Go find your real copilot.* That spoke to me. My ego was so busy assigning blame, it was keeping me from choosing my own happiness.

"There's no reason to talk shit about your ex, Jon," he continued. "You're a growth-motivated person, and she couldn't help you grow. It didn't work out. You know how many guys I see who are married and in their forties and feel stuck? Send her a bottle of Johnnie Walker Blue and thank her. And guess what? You'll be free, close that chapter, have forgiveness, and then go find that woman who wants to fly with you throughout life."

Within an hour, I felt myself returning to me. Elko had reminded me of who I was, and how I'd lost track of myself. Leaving Big Dom's office, I popped my shades on and the old bounce in my step had returned. *I'm back, baby.*

The first thing I did after reaching closure over my divorce was change all my passwords to *freeatlast*. That was me, telling myself a story about my new reality. It was also how I felt: I was young, playing in the National Football League, and I was going to enjoy those two facts for a while.

Maybe it's because my family was ripped from me at such an early age, but even in macho locker rooms, I'd always been the sensitive guy. Remember that journal I kept as a twelve- and thirteen-year-old? Well, I picked it back up at seventeen, when I'd met a girl. Reading it today finds an earnest, lovelorn voice:

> *My feelings for Amanda are new to me, for I've never felt this way about anyone before. She's beautiful, cunning, smart . . . but I see a little girl inside her that I don't think has ever been seen before . . . Holding her meant more than words can describe. A gentle caress and a smile. I know what I want. I want her to believe in me like I believe in her.*

That's still kinda me today. I cry at chick flicks. Like, seriously. *Notting Hill?* When Julia Roberts, looking at Hugh Grant, tells the assembled press she'll be staying in Britain "indefinitely" to be with him . . . well, that gets me every time.

After my divorce, though, I was having *casual* relationships. I wasn't treating anyone badly, mind you. But I was probably licking my wounds and shying away from being emotionally vulnerable again. I also didn't want the responsibility of worrying about anyone else. If I wanted to do something, I just wanted to do it. After my divorce, I took a vacation to Aruba—by myself, and I loved every second of it.

One day, my buddy Tim Mooney called. To refer to Tim as a "buddy" is an understatement. He's been a mentor and father figure. I met him when I was playing for the Eagles. He does a lot for charity, and through a buddy, his request had come to me: he knew a ten-year-old kid who was dying of testicular cancer who loved the Eagles. Could I get him in to see a game? I could do more than that. I had Tim and the kid and his dad on the field prior to kickoff. The kid idolized wide receiver DeSean Jackson, and when I brought DeSean over to meet him, the kid's eyes widened and he damn near started hyperventilating. Moments like those—seeing pure joy spread across a kid's face, when joy would seem to be in such short supply—that's what makes playing in the NFL worthwhile. Afterward, Mooney, a big, backslapping kind of guy, approached me with tears in his eyes.

I thought, *This is one cool dude.* A guy's guy, like me, with a huge heart. He asked me to host an auction he puts on in Atlantic City to benefit the Atlantic County Special Services School District. I did the benefit, only when it came time to select the winner of the grand prize—a first-class trip to the Bahamas worth thousands of dollars—I reached into a bowl and picked . . . my own damn name. That ain't right. So I disqualified myself, auctioned off the vacation, and raised another $6,000 for the charity.

"You won fair and square," Mooney protested. But no, I didn't like the way that looked; the emcee shouldn't win the grand prize. "Man, all I can tell you," Mooney said, giving in, "is you're my guy."

And he wasn't kidding. I joined the board of his charity—he raises money for special-needs kids—and he mentors me in life, using his vast hookups throughout the entertainment and casino businesses. He's a daily sounding board, the ultimate cornerman.

Now he was calling with what would turn out to be a life-changing offer. "Hey, Jon," Mooney said. "I got this chick I want you to meet."

"Cool," I said, nonchalant. "But for the record, I'm not looking for anything serious." He laughed, because he'd heard it before. After my divorce, I'd told him, "If you ever hear me say the word 'marriage' again, punch me square in the face."

Now he had a girl for me. "She's looking for love, and she's got a great spirit," he said.

The new "playa" in me wanted to get right to the facts. "What's she look like? What does she do?"

"She works in Vegas at one of the casinos," Mooney said. "She's a six-foot blonde."

I paused. "I'm good, Mooney, thanks," I said. "The last thing I need is a six-foot hoochie mama from Vegas."

Mooney explained she was actually a casino executive. But I wasn't hearing it. Remember, I was in my self-centered stage. I wasn't treating women with disrespect, but I had a newly cold attitude about dating: I'm divorced, I've got a good job, I've got time, and I don't answer to nobody. It may have been a lonely life, but it was easy. This chick might be complicated.

Meantime, unbeknownst to me, Mooney was encountering some pushback from her about me. She'd been telling him that in Vegas, there were no guys for a woman in her thirties who was looking to fall in love. "Annalise," he said. "I've got this great guy for you to meet."

"Really? What's he do?" she asked.

"He plays in the NFL," Mooney said, and the hammer came down almost before the words had left his lips.

"Hell no, he's a douchebag," she said. "I've dealt with athletes before. And I hear stories. I don't need that. I'm good."

She was even more put off when Mooney explained that I was recently divorced and not looking for anything serious. But Mooney is one persistent dude. He stayed on both of us until we agreed to a phone call.

Her name was Annalise Davis—Anni ("Ah-knee") for short—and her title was customer development executive at MGM Resorts International in Vegas. So much for being a bimbo. In our call, she was funny. And accomplished, but not stuck-up. That led to another call. Man, she was bright. That led to a third. She was positive—there was no "woe is me" in her story.

Before either of us knew it, we were talking *every* day. Then multiple times a day. Nine or ten hours a day. We'd both curl up in bed and fall asleep with the other's voice in our ear. Looking back on it now, we're grateful we didn't meet online or on Tinder. Neither of us was ever performing for the other. We were just two voices on either side of the country, connecting through a phone line. Really connecting. To this day, Anni is the only person I've ever been *totally* myself with. Like, the disgusting jokes in the locker room? Most guys don't share that stuff with their wives. For me, something didn't really happen until I *could* share it with her.

Our talking went on for three months. Once, we started talking about what our dream first date would be. "Wait, don't tell me," I said. "Let's hang up and text each other what it would be—otherwise, you'll hear mine, and just agree."

Sure enough, we texted each other damn near the exact same date. I said I'd want to cruise the harbor in a shitty boat together, listen to music and grab some tacos from Chronic Tacos, and laugh for hours. No alcohol. No fancy restaurant. Hers? She wanted to walk on the beach, eat an ice cream cone, and just talk and laugh.

Finally, I couldn't stand it any longer. "Listen, I've had enough of the phone thing," I said. "I'm coming to Vegas and we're going to dinner."

Finally, the time had come. The disembodied voice took real form in front of me. When I first laid eyes on Anni, I was surprised. I knew she'd be blond and six feet tall, but what I hadn't anticipated was how her smile lit her—and everything around her—up. Some people have infectious smiles. I couldn't imagine ever being sad around her.

I got a hotel room, but we agreed beforehand that we wouldn't get it on. If this thing worked, we didn't want to have a kid conceived in a Vegas hotel room our first night together. So what did we do? We had dinner in Vegas and then went to my place in Southern California, where we enacted *both of* our dream first dates. We took a Duffy boat through Newport Harbor and then walked the beach with ice cream cones. (Which, when Anni wasn't looking, I promptly threw up, because I'm lactose intolerant. Good times.)

That week, Anni had a work event in Southern California. So our weekend continued back at my house in Huntington Beach. We held hands walking along the ocean, right near the spot where I talk to Mom. Anni listened to the whole story and held me when the emotion rose.

At the end of our time together, I went to LAX. I'd be heading to Boston to perform, and she was going to San Diego. Before takeoff, I called her while she was driving south. "Yo," she said. "What are we doing?"

"I don't know," I said.

I'll never forget this: "I think we're going to regret not seeing where this goes," she said.

Sometimes, doing nothing is the wisest course of action. This wasn't one of those times. I blurted out exactly what I was feeling inside. "You know what? You're right," I said. "Do you wanna move in with me?"

There was hardly a pause. "Yes," she said. "I love my job, I worked my whole life for it, but I have no problem quitting to move in with you, because I think you're the love of my life."

"I think you're mine," I said.

The only thing left to do was FaceTime Mooney.

"Hey, man, how'd it go?" he said, thinking he was about to get a down and dirty debrief from his bro.

"Oh, man, it was awesome," I said. "We hung out for days, we laughed, we cried, it was just amazing. She's moving in next week."

There was a pause, like he was trying to gauge whether I was busting on him. "What now?" he said.

"Yeah, we're moving in together," I said.

"Dude, you were just supposed to hang out!" he said.

Later, Anni told Mooney that he'd better apply for some universal minister accreditation—because when we got married, he'd be conducting the service. "I can't believe you guys," he said, laughing. "You're crazy!"

Crazy is right. But Anni diving all in? How freakin' rock-star is that?

Less than two years later, there we were, Anni and me, dressed in all white in our barefoot beach wedding ceremony in Cabo. We rented out the posh Cabo del Sol golf resort, so we had a thousand yards of private beach, surrounded by peninsula.

I was in a white suit with an open shirt, and Anni looked smokin' in a white Galia Lahav wedding dress. There was Mooney, all in white, too, officiating the service. All my boys were there, too—a point of personal pride that the dudes I'd played *Bad News Bears* baseball with back in the day under Coach Eckles were my groomsmen at *both* my weddings. Bros for life.

It was us, and the eighty most important people in our lives.

We were introduced with a remix of Marvin Gaye's "Let's Get It On" and we surprised everyone with some cool fireworks on the beach. Everything just felt so right and so easy.

Standing on that beach, holding Anni's hands and looking deeply into her eyes, I couldn't stop thinking about what she'd done for me. It may sound crazy or corny, but she was my savior. "There was an emptiness inside me," I told her. "And you turned my heart right side up."

I'd never been with someone who so clearly thought the best of me. With Anni, both of us were in every moment, together.

I'd have never seen the pure goodness in her, though, if I'd remained bitter about my past. If I were still resentful—whether toward my dad or my ex or whomever—I would have never seen Anni's true heart. That's what depressed people do: they don't see other people in their life clearly because they're too lost in their own depression or bitterness. It's an endless feedback loop: you're depressed, your self-talk fuels your depression, and it all colors how you approach everyone around you.

But what I'd learned is that how you view and talk to yourself is the same way you view and talk to the world. Once I'd forgiven and moved on, I could see Anni for who she really was: the most kind, giving, loving person I'd ever known.

That day, on that beach, was the happiest day of my life, not just because I was getting married, but because I'd worked my way to the certainty that, every day, I was one day closer to the person I wanted to be. And now that person had what he had always craved: a soul mate who was a partner in adventure for life.

Elko, man, what a prophet. Sure enough, I'd found that person who would fly through life with me. My copilot. We'd be in for some bumpy rides. But we'd take on the turbulence, together.

CHAPTER TWELVE

"Don't Hate. Don't Blame. Forgive."

Doubt kills more dreams than failure ever will.
—Suzy Kassem

Oh, snap. I'm in over my head.

It was the spring of 2016, and my friend Cris Judd had encouraged me to audition for *America's Got Talent*. *What the hell*, I thought, *may as well give it a shot*. I had the time. Off-season practices weren't starting for a couple of weeks—I'd audition, hopefully get Simon and the judges to say some positive things that I could use as quotes to promote my speaking career. Then I'd opt out of the show or get eliminated, and head to Philly to be a football player again. No reason to even tell the Eagles. It was all a lark.

So there I was, in an auditorium packed with two thousand people, all there to see performers hoping to get their big break. I didn't know what to expect. In one of the early rounds, I was standing in the wings of the theater and I could have sworn I saw some magician float, grow wings, and turn into a bird. I was a little intimidated.

"What the hell just happened? Did that dude just fly away?"

I said to Anni, looking at *my* props—a jumbo deck of cards, a Sharpie, and a pad of paper in my hand. "I think I picked the wrong routine."

This is why I love this girl. At moments of doubt, she promptly reminds me of my story. "Are you kidding me?" she said. "You'll be fine. Just be yourself. Your talent is relating to the audience and making them feel special."

She was right, of course. I'd never thought of myself as Mr. Magician Guy. My magic was more a means to an end, a way to connect. When I'm cooking onstage, it's one big party. 'Cause, for me, magic ain't about the trick; it's about the fun. I don't want the audience to think I *really* possess magical powers. I want them to want to hang with me because they're going to laugh their asses off and be moved.

Now I really had *two* audiences: the folks in the seats in the studio *and* the judges. I had to win over Howie Mandel, Heidi Klum, Mel B, and—most of all—Simon Cowell.

"You don't have to create a fan base," Elko had told me years ago, when he was counseling me on how to build my motivational-speaker brand. "You can tap into fan bases that already exist."

Back then, it meant that I could build my brand by combining some Buffalo Bills fans with, say, some of Elko's corporate clientele. Now, I realized, the same advice applied. Each of the judges had fans who tuned in to *AGT* just to see them. If I could get each judge on my side, I'd get their fans pulling for me, too.

That meant including the judges in my act. Let other magicians try to blow them away with pyrotechnics. If my fifty-two buddies and I could get each of the judges to laugh and to drop their jaws, if their fans could see them loving me, and me loving them . . . well, I'd be golden.

That's what I set out to do, starting with my first appearance on *AGT*, the audition. With nothing but a deck of cards, I strode onto that stage. Howie's a sports guy, so he recognized my name right away. "You play for the Philadelphia Eagles!" he said.

That was cool, but there was a possible downside, too. Historically, Simon was the toughest judge. I didn't want him thinking I was some football meathead who hacked magic. If anything, I'm *more* passionate about my magic than about my football. "Let me ask you a question," Simon said. "This goes well, you win, then what do you do?"

"Well, let's be honest," I said. "The NFL stands for Not For Long, so I've been lucky here. You've always gotta have a backup plan, and this is a pretty good one, you know what I'm saying?"

Howie, laughing, said, "Show us your magic."

"Let's rock this out," I said, and then made those judges mine. I had Heidi choose a random card, facedown, and we folded it and place-marked it in front of Mel B with a paper clip. Then, with each judge yelling out "Stop" while I shuffled, I removed from the deck cards numbered in order from ace to king. "The number one trick from a comedy magician is to pull it out of your—" I said, seeming to pull a three from my butt, to much laughter.

With each reveal, the judges and audience members gasped. They were randomly picking these cards—how could they be coming out sequentially? I asked Simon to think of any card. "Three of clubs," he said.

Then I shuffled all of the cards into their four different suits—more oohs and aahs from the audience—and then called everyone's attention to the card we started with in front of Mel B, the folded one with the paper clip. It was handed to Simon.

As he opened it, I narrated: "The card you thought of—the three of clubs!" I said.

Simon kept holding that card up, dumbfounded. "You're bewildered!" Howie said. "Simon, use words!"

"I don't know what to say," he said. "I don't know how the hell you did that. I could see it never moved. For someone who doesn't do this professionally, it was so slick, so fast, the dialogue was great. It's not a trick because it's magic. It was amazing. I'm really impressed."

Man, I was beaming. All the judges voted me on to the next round—the Judge Cuts—but not before Howie said, "I just want to say something. You have a gift, and it's the gift of making magic happen—for you and for others."

Heidi chimed in: "I loved it, you're fast with your hands, you're fast with your mouth, you're charming."

Talk about validation. Anni had predicted it. When Heidi called me charming, it meant I'd gotten her and the other judges—and, by extension, the audience—*invested*. They cared. And when she commented on the speed of my hands, it reminded me just how much I owed Anni. The old me would have recoiled at the thought of anyone looking at my hands, because of their gnarly state, thanks to my constant biting. But Anni's presence in my life had cured me of that habit. That's why the coolest thing about my *America's Got Talent* run was that my two favorite girls were in the audience for every show: Anni and my aunt Susan, as well as my grandparents.

The next round, I performed a trick from my act. A deck of cards drawn on a notepad magically comes to life as a real deck of cards; rising from the notebook page is the card that guest judge Ne-Yo had picked from the deck. But when I ripped the page off the notebook and handed it to a stunned Ne-Yo, the card and deck were once again just drawn on the page. There was no hole where the card had previously risen from. Howie catapulted into a standing ovation, and Ne-Yo was flabbergasted. He hit the Golden Buzzer in front of him, and all hell broke loose: confetti streamed down, Susan, Anni, and my grandparents jumped into each other's arms. It meant I was getting a pass to advance straight into the quarterfinals.

It was all a rush, and it was super cool. But now things were getting complicated. See, we'd taped the first two rounds while it was still my off-season. But now training camp was starting and the show was about to air—which meant the Eagles would find out I'd been moonlighting. Worse, beginning with the quarterfinals, the show would be broadcast live. Which was scheduled during training camp. Uh-oh.

Bouncing up the steps to the Eagles training facility at the start of camp, I saw four figures in the lobby. They were too small, and too well dressed, to be players. As I got closer, it was as I'd feared: there was team owner Jeffrey Lurie, team president Don Smolenski, CFO Frank Gumienny, and general manager Howie Roseman. All waiting for me.

They weren't pissed, though, about my *AGT* appearances. Get this: they were there to congratulate me. "Why didn't you tell us?" Jeffrey wanted to know.

"Well, I didn't expect to get the Golden Buzzer and make it to the quarterfinals," I said.

"Well, what are you going to do now?" he asked.

"I'm gonna just opt out," I said. "I'm ready to play me some football."

They all looked at each other. Jeffrey—who'd invited me to his wedding and who had told me I was family—clearly didn't like my answer. He's someone, like me, who is all heart. I don't think he could stomach it if someone who worked for him were denied pursuing a dream because of his job. "Can't we figure out a way to make this work?" he said. "Magic is a big part of your life, and you're a big part of this organization. We should be able to make this work."

The other guys were nodding in agreement. I choked up. Why

should they go the extra mile like this, for me? A freakin' long snapper? Jeffrey, as if reading my mind, offered that it was *because* I'm just a long snapper that they'd want to do this. "It's not like you're the quarterback," he said, laughing.

When someone is paying you $1.1 million a year to snap a weirdly shaped ball through your legs, you kinda don't want to say to them, "You know what? I'll catch up with you guys later." But here was the management of our team, saying, *Go chase your dream. We got you.* How cool is that?

There's a lot of coldness in professional sports. As a player, you quickly learn that the game you've played your whole life is really a business with little room for sentiment. The Eagles, after all, are a multibillion-dollar franchise. But after Jeffrey fired Chip Kelly, he talked publicly and to the team about the importance of emotional intelligence in the workplace. I think he saw the *AGT* opportunity as an example of that: helping me chase my dream, as long as it didn't interfere with the team's on-field performance, was actually smart business—because it was the team saying to me and to my teammates, *We've got your back. What's important to you is important to us.* It's what I learned under Coach Reid. You want employees to bust through brick walls for you? Show them you're in their corner.

So I started the craziest damn work commute you've ever heard of. I'd duck out after our special-teams meeting at 5:00 p.m. and hop on a flight to LA. I'd get to the *AGT* soundstage, rehearse for a couple of hours, and then make the red eye back to Philly and get to training camp for the team meeting by 8:00 a.m. How crazy is that? Of course, it would only last until we taped this next round, and then I'd be sent packing, right?

Before that, the second-round appearance aired, and the coolest part was that I was able to share with millions what Susan had done for me and Krissy. "My mom's sister, who is sitting right there, gave up her entire life, did everything she could to fight for custody of my sister and me," I said from the stage while the TV cameras focused in on Susan. In the prerecorded setup piece, there was Susan: "I always say the worst tragedy of my life became my greatest gift," she said.

Think about what Susan did: she was thirty-two. She was single. Her whole life was in front of her. And she essentially became a mom to two kids. How can you ever thank someone for making *you* the most important thing in her life? It almost seems like you can't. Like it's *beyond* thanks. That's how I'd always felt, that the best way of showing my gratitude was to make Susan—and Mom—proud of the man I'd become. But sharing with others the story of just what she'd done—the sacrifice she'd made out of such deep love? Man, that felt good. Honestly, if you told me I had a choice: share with the millions of viewers Susan's story *or* go on to the next round, I wouldn't have hesitated: *Get that camera on my aunt's beautiful face.* That's the *real* magic.

This time, in *AGT*'s pretaped setup piece before the quarterfinal appearance, Nonnie and Poppy were interviewed on camera. "Oh my gosh, magic was the cure," Nonnie said, remembering the sad twelve-year-old who, she said, would "take his sweatshirt and just rub it and say, 'I don't have a mom anymore.'"

As with Susan the previous round, win or lose, *America's Got Talent* was affording me the opportunity to pay props to my Nonnie and Poppy. "My grandpa wasn't a magician by trade," I told a national audience. "But he taught me that something can be so difficult but if I just work on it and practice it, I'll figure it out."

The show also enabled me to make Kathy Dorenbos immortal, just like she is to me: "Magic? It's guided me, and to me, that's my mom saying 'I'm right here, in the front row, and I love you,'"

I said. "She is the light that shines on me. Every day of my life, I know my mom is there."

Remember how, when the Bills first signed me, Coach Gregg Williams said he wasn't worried about me falling to pieces if I had a bad snap? What he was really saying was that owing to what I'd gone through, I could handle pressure. Well, so it was now. I wasn't feeling any pressure during the *AGT* run. Instead, what I was feeling was vast amounts of gratitude. Are you kidding me? Getting the opportunity to be beamed into living rooms across the United States and introduce folks to amazing people like Krissy, Susan, Nonnie, Poppy, Mom, and Annalise? That's priceless, man. I wanted to win, sure, but I'd *already* won.

Starting with the quarterfinal round, all *AGT* shows would now feature live voting by the TV audience. By now, I knew the routine. You have no contact with the judges prior to taking the stage—they want to be totally fresh to the experience of you. But I was starting to feel like I'd won Simon and the others over. My doubts about whether I belonged were long gone.

This time, I came out with a prediction in a bottle, and set it right next to Simon. After asking each of the judges to draw something on poster board and to keep it facedown, I precisely predicted what each had drawn—and then unveiled what, in that bottle, was a pretty close replica of Simon's very odd drawing of a dog. The crowd went nuts, and Simon was again caught off guard. "It was magic, because it was right in front of me," he said. "He didn't touch anything. No one's drawn my dog like that. You know what, Jon? I think you are a great guy, a great American hero, a real superstar. I think America is going to get behind you."

With an endorsement like that from the famously fickle Simon, the votes came flowing in. I didn't have time to celebrate, though. We'd done the show live, from 5:00 till 7:00 p.m., Pacific time.

I hustled to LAX and got a red eye so I could make the 8:00 a.m. team meeting. Talk about magic.

Now it was on to the semifinals, where I connected the trick to football. I'd constructed a big Velcro map of the United States on set and I asked each judge to snap or throw a Velcro football at the board. The four footballs landed on four different states. Next, I revealed a set of quarters inside a small treasure chest. When the judges read the backs of the four quarters, they found them engraved with the very states they'd hit with their footballs. Not only that, inside one of my journals that I assigned Howie to guard with his life was a map of the states that included the judges' photos on the very states they'd just randomly hit with their footballs.

Now I'd definitely won Simon over. "Can I say something, Jon?" he said, holding and inspecting the map that had been in the journal. "This was the most incredible thing I've ever seen on one of these shows. I absolutely love the fact, Jon, that you've come here with a successful career but you've come here to win. That's what I love about you. You had very little time to do this, you had to get the whole thing together, it was chaotic, and I'm watching this in front of me. I think you are a genius."

The votes were in. It was on to the finals. But first, I had practice in the morning.

In sports, there's a saying: *Dance with the one that brung ya*. It reflects the conventional wisdom: if you're a running team that pounds away at the defensive line, you double down on that at crunch time—you don't stop doing what got you to the Super Bowl once you make it to the big game. Well, as I strategized about the *AGT* finals, I thought, counterintuitively, *Screw conventional wisdom*.

• • •

It was 9:52 at night. I know, because for some reason, I looked at the clock when it happened. I was sitting at the kitchen table in my condo in South Philly, just a few city blocks from the Linc, the stadium where I plied my *other* trade.

I was huddled over a notepad. Now I *was* feeling the pressure like there were only a few ticks left on the clock before a do-or-die field-goal attempt. I was trying to prepare something new and different for the *AGT* finals . . . and that inner voice of doubt in my head had returned. It was the voice I'd spent so long training myself to tune out on the football field.

Until now, my *AGT* appearances had been frenzied and full of energy, just like my act. Partly that was because I liked to keep moving when performing because, before being saved by Anni, I never wanted anyone to catch a glimpse of the disgusting state of my nails.

But I also try to be the Springsteen of magic—every trick like it's an ultra-energetic finale—because it's also about pure adrenaline. Remember, I was drawn to football not for the game but for the absolute rush of bursting out of the locker room onto a field before a hundred thousand shrieking, screaming fans. I always wanted to be a rock star—to experience the excitement of a moment with an arena full of fellow human beings. Rockers bare their soul. Now it was my turn.

But now I was thinking of doing it in a much more deliberate way. Magic had been a lonely, scared boy's companion and salvation. I used it to find myself; now, on the eve of the finals, writing my script, I realized it was a chance to talk about what magic had meant to me.

To do that meant slowing down my act. My performance would still be a rock-star moment, but I've always loved acoustic music—and this would be my ballad. My playing cards were my guitar. The stage was America.

Only now, sitting at that kitchen table, I knew what I wanted to do . . . but the words weren't coming. Anni and my buddy Anthony were sitting with me when the doubts returned. I flung the cards onto the table in front of me. "I don't think this is going to be good enough to win," I said.

I was staring intently at the cards when I heard a thud behind me.

"Jon . . ." Anni said. In retrospect, there was some trepidation in her voice, but it didn't register then. I was too focused on the self-doubt I'd just heard from myself.

I said nothing.

"Honey, you're going to want to see this," Anni said hesitantly. Something in her voice made me turn. There, on the floor, was the photo of Mom and me that had, up till now, never moved from the secure shelf above, where it had sat for years. Looking up to me from the floor was my mom; when the picture was taken, she was roughly the age I was at that moment. Mom looked back at me with those wide eyes, so full of love, and that kindest of kind smiles. I could almost hear her full-throated laugh—she was so full of joy—in our collective silence.

All three of us stared at Mom's photo on the ground. "Jon, that picture came down right when you said maybe this isn't the right act," Anni said, tearing up. "I think there's your answer."

Whoa. *Things just got real deep real quick*, I remember thinking. I felt a lump forming in my throat, and soon the tears welled up. I'd been wrestling with revealing *me*—not Jon Dorenbos, football player, or Jon Dorenbos, comedian/magician—in the finale, slowing down and allowing myself to be vulnerable and open about life and how to get through it, while performing my sleights of hand. Sure, I've done a lot of things other people might consider scary, including flying airplanes and being chased around by, and chasing, hulking giants on the football field, but, c'mon, we know that behind the fear of every courageous act lurks some other insecurity. So there I was, doubting my instinct to open up the love in my heart before a national audience . . . and there was Mom, rattling my cage, as if to say, *Go for it, Jonny.*

I know what some dudes in the locker room would say. "C'mon, man, a picture fell off a shelf. How do you know there's a message in that?" All I can point to is what happened next. Anni and I hugged. Anthony poured me a Tito's and Seven and we clanked our drinks together. I took a long pull and sat back down. And then the words just came streaming out of me, as if they were coming from some force greater than me.

A few days later, I played against the Cleveland Browns in our season home opener. We won, 29–10. As soon as the game ended, I didn't even have time to shake hands at midfield. I sprinted into the locker room, quickly changed, met up with Anni, and we hustled to the airport to get to LA. I had a show to do.

The act I performed during the finals of *AGT* reproduced the exact words that flowed out of me that night in my condo, a slow jam cowritten by Mom, inspired by all the advice I'd soaked up from Kevin Elko over the years.

The first thing I did was ask Heidi, Mel B, and Howie to sign three cards. Back into the deck they went. Then I asked Simon to write on his card the name of someone who meant a lot to him and to share it with us. He wrote "Eric," his son's name, and his card joined the others. Then, with no background music, the camera came in close on my hands, and I began shuffling while narrating my story.

"I wanted to take an opportunity to tell America what magic has meant to me," I said, shuffling until those autographed cards from each of the judges appeared seemingly out of nowhere. "Magic saved my life. There have been plenty of times when I was lost and I didn't have the answers and I didn't know where to go.

So what I did is I turned to magic and it helped me find myself. It simply taught me: Don't hate. Don't blame. And forgive.

"This is life," I said, shuffling my fifty-two bros. "When everything is going so perfect and yet tragedy and chaos, they strike when we least expect it . . . We all face this. But I think the difference is, do we decide, and do we choose to live in vision or do we live in circumstance? And I don't know about you guys, but I wake up every single morning and I choose to live in vision, to find happiness knowing that life will work its way out and we will find ourselves."

The magic, I said, is not in my hands. It's in each one of us. "Simon, you wrote the name 'Eric,'" I said, holding up his card, standing before a backward chalkboard that had been on the stage since I walked onto it. "I thought I'd make a little to-do list for you. Every night, may the magic forever live in your home."

Here I slowly turned the chalkboard around; on it, was written the word "Eric." "Grab your son and tell Eric you love him," I said. "And cross that off your list every night. And, ladies and gentlemen, may this world be magic. I love you!"

Simon jumped up, a look of wonder on his face, and the audience followed. I'd slowed things down and expressed what's deep in my soul: that we're all on a journey to find ourselves. When we went to commercial, a stunning woman, likely in her early forties, jumped up onstage from the audience and grabbed the cards the judges had signed. I approached her, thinking she was some kind of autograph collector, looking to swipe the cards to make a quick buck.

But then she put down the cards signed by Howie, Mel B, and Heidi. And she held the one on which Simon had written "Eric."

She looked at me, and I noticed that she was clearly moved. All of a sudden Simon was next to her, his arm around her waist. "Eric is my son," she said. "Would you mind if I kept this and hang it in our home, as a reminder that the world is magic?"

So this was Lauren Silverman, Simon's partner and mother to Eric, who was then two years old. "Of course," I said, opening my arms to hug her.

There was a lot of hugging going on that night. I didn't win the voting—the title went to a young girl who played the ukulele. Of the ten finalists, I received the third-highest total of votes.

Of course, I had wanted to win. I didn't. But I knew it was way easier to accept losing when you've given everything you've got. And I did. The other competitors—amazing performers—were full of praise for me. I guess Coach Hay was right: win the respect of your opponents and you will win far more than you will lose. Though I lost *America's Got Talent*, I won in so many ways.

I felt prouder of this performance than any I'd ever done. By 10:30 Pacific time, I was on that red eye back to Philly, on the way to make that 8:00 a.m. meeting. Up in those clouds, I thought a lot about Mom, my cowriter. And I couldn't help but think: *I wonder if Dad watched this?*

CHAPTER THIRTEEN

Making History

People will forget what you said, people will forget what you did, but people will never forget how you made them feel.
                                        —Maya Angelou

My most excellent *AGT* adventure led to a new national profile for me. Outside of Philly, I was quick to learn, most people who knew of me now knew me as a magician—not as a football player. That was pretty cool, and represented a sea change in my career. It was the first time that, nationally, magic was so widely associated with me—just as I'd always dreamed it would be.

Even on the field, the *AGT* experience was never far from the surface. Once, playing the Green Bay Packers, we had just punted and I was heading off when I saw Packers quarterback Aaron Rodgers running over to me near our sideline. I thought he was lost and I was about to say, *Dude, turn around, your huddle is that way*, when he got up real close and put his arm around me. "You were awesome on *America's Got Talent*," he said. "I had so much fun watching you. I really dug the positive message you sent."

Pretty cool. At the line of scrimmage, though, comments tended not to be quite so complimentary. I made it a policy to never talk trash to guys who were bigger and stronger than me,

159

particularly if they'd soon be lining up across from me. Why make some dude angry when he's about to try to hurt you anyway?

I made one exception, though. Once, just before a snap, a giant of a man across from me said, "Magic man! Gonna make you disappear, magic man! That you, magic man? Say good-bye, magic man!"

I'm usually not this quick. "Yeah, that's me, the magic man," I said. "Who the fuck are you?"

Man, his *own* teammates burst out laughing. "Oh, snap, he got you! He got you!" they yelled, just before the snap.

Meantime, I got a call from *The Ellen DeGeneres Show*. Ellen loves magic and really loved the "don't hate, don't blame, and forgive" *AGT* finale. Would I come on to perform? Uh, *would* I? Hells, yes. I'd always *loved* Ellen and considered her a kindred spirit. You want to talk positive energy? That comes naturally to Ellen. Plus, she's funny as hell, and I've always believed that those two qualities go hand in hand. You *can't* be positive without being joyful. I'd long been a regular viewer of Ellen's TV show—and there weren't a lot of people at the Eagles training facility asking for the channel to be switched from *SportsCenter* to *Ellen* on the communal TV. Now I was going to have the chance to meet and perform for her.

Of course, we were now in season. But I was a veteran of this commute. I hopped a flight to LA on a Monday, knowing I needed to make it back in time for practice on Wednesday. Once there, I learned that Ellen approaches her show the same way the *AGT* judges approach theirs. She wasn't at rehearsal because she wanted to experience the show live with her audience. Before arriving, I watched some old clips of magicians who had appeared on her show, searching for ways I could stand out.

For one thing, none brought my level of energy to their act. From the first moments of Ellen's show, when everybody is up and dancing, it's a party. You can't talk in a monotone and be all controlled. *I've gotta be the life of this party*, I thought. But also, Ellen's all about being positive and helping people. Well, so am I, so it just made sense for the magic I did on her show to fit that theme.

The typical magician might ask a randomly chosen audience member to write down their celebrity fantasy—and then, lo and behold, reveal that he'd predicted that very scenario: *"You want to go to Tahiti with George Clooney!"* Well, George Clooney and Tahiti are cool, but kinda lame for a reveal in a magic trick. But I liked the concept. So, tailoring it to our vibe—Ellen's and mine—I asked four random audience members to express how Ellen has changed their lives and what she meant to them, while Ellen wrote their key words on some hanging poster boards. Wouldn't you know it? I'd predicted those very words beforehand, and unveiled the same sentiments on my very own piece of paper, leaving Ellen with a stunned look on her face. But to me, the key wasn't the trick; the key was actually *using* the trick to further the connection between Ellen and her fans. Through my magic, Ellen's fans got a chance to tell her they loved her.

From that moment on, Ellen and I were tight. During another visit, I revealed that with the snap of my fingers, a card Ellen had just torn apart was somehow all in one piece again right in the palm of her hand.

"Just like you make us feel every day, we come together," I said to her. "We feel whole and we feel like new—just because of you. We love you."

"You're crazy!" she shouted, wide-eyed. "I love you!"

I stood next to Ellen in my Eagles number 46 jersey when she closed the show, which she always ends with her trademark reminder, "Be kind to one another."

First, though, she reminded *me* of something else: "You're so good at this," she said. "I can't believe you're really a football player."

Oh, yeah, *that*.

• • •

I'd continue making regular appearances on *Ellen*; I'd kind of become her house magician. But meantime, as Ellen reminded me, I had football games to win. The Eagles were under first-year head coach Doug Pederson, a great dude who had been an assistant under ol' Big Red. We were up and down throughout the 2016–17 season, and would eventually finish seven-and-nine, but there was one glowing reason for optimism: our rookie quarterback, Carson Wentz.

Remember how struck I was when I first joined the Eagles by the leadership abilities of backup quarterback Jeff Garcia? Well, take Garcia's ability to get guys to follow his example and combine it with the physical skills of someone who is six-foot-five, who runs like a gazelle, and whose arm strength is otherworldly, and you've got Wentz.

The Eagles had traded up in the NFL draft to pick him with the second overall pick, and from the moment Carson walked into the locker room, I could tell it had been the right move. Some guys just have it. Carson carried himself with a swagger, but his demeanor was more quiet and infectiously confident than obnoxious and "look at me." In fact, he was a humble, God-fearing kid who just loved the game and loved his teammates. Out on the field, he was tough as nails. I'd been around long enough to know that if you have a quarterback like this, someone with the whole package, including those all-important leadership qualities, you were going places.

So I was newly psyched about the future of our team, and my place on it. I'd survived so long in the cutthroat NFL because I expected to be cut every year. I had no right to expect anything more from this game that had already given me so much. There was no pressure, no ego. Just me, the ball, and the moment. But a couple of cool things happened as this season—my fourteenth in the league—went on.

First, the NFL Network and writer/producer Mark Kriegel broadcast a piece on me in which I bared my soul. There were scenes of me at Mom's grave, wearing a hoodie in the dead of night, telling her I love her, my voice crackling. Off the air, Kriegel contacted my dad to see if he'd sit for an interview. I knew that Dad had been out of jail for over a decade by then, but that's all I knew. Kriegel tracked him down and told me later that Dad said he wishes me well and he'd only speak if all three of his kids said it was okay. I thought that was pretty cool of him.

Shortly thereafter, the Eagles nominated me for the Walter Payton NFL Man of the Year Award, which each year honors a player's charity work. Just to have my name mentioned in the same breath as Walter Payton's, someone who was not only a great player but also a great humanitarian, was super humbling. I was a dude who finagled his way into a college scholarship, who snapped a ball through his legs, and who never thought he'd last in the league. Now, fourteen years in, I was finally getting the message that maybe I belonged, after all.

Which is why Week 13 of our season mattered so much. We were playing Washington at home. We had fading playoff hopes, but the game held more significance than that for me. It would actually be my 162nd consecutive regular-season game for the Eagles, tying a franchise record held by All-Pro wide receiver Harold Carmichael, who'd had the record for damn near twenty-five years.

Since I'd come into the league, my goal had been to be the oldest guy on my team. That's what I'd say to myself when bench-pressing: *Last man standing!* Longevity had come to mean everything to me. It meant I'd shown up for my brothers in the locker room, week after week. And it meant that the guy signing my checks could count on me, week after week.

Woody Allen once said that "eighty percent of life is showing up," and I showed up, even when it was difficult, like when I tore those ligaments in my ankle and had to move in to the trainer's room for a week to rehab around the clock in order to play on Sunday. Then there was the time I had a migraine headache and diarrhea when we were playing the Seahawks in Seattle. During snaps, I had to concentrate on just not soiling myself. I can't tell you how many hits I took over the years that left my body feeling like it had been in a ten-car pileup on the freeway. But not playing was never an option. And that wasn't just due to personal pride or stubbornness or ego. It was because I felt *obligated*. To my teammates and my employer. If my team is crazy enough to pay me a million bucks a year to bend over and snap a ball through my legs, I'm sure as hell gonna show up and do everything I can to be the best at it.

Now, 162 games pales in comparison to 2,632, which is how many consecutive games iron man Cal Ripken Jr. played in baseball. It's hard to wrap your head around that number. But I always thought that was one of the coolest records in sports. In part, it's because people can relate to the value of just showing up. I remember hearing Ripken talk about how many fans would come up to him and share their *own* stories—kids who went a whole school year without an absence, factory workers who never left the floor. There's dignity in the simple act of showing up to work no matter what you do for a living.

As the record-tying game approached, it was those folks I found myself thinking of. I thought of what my former teammate Brian Dawkins had said that helped me come back from that ankle injury: every fan in the stands would trade places with me in a heartbeat. The least I could do was freakin' show up and do my job.

Early in the second half of the game against the Redskins, I was covering a kick and got blocked from behind. Nothing was called, but Coach Pederson later said it was an illegal block. Anyway, because I'm an unathletic white dude, it sent me flailing with my arms out. That's when the freakiest thing happened. My right arm was fully extended at the exact moment my teammate Bryan Braman just happened to be running by—at full speed. My hand met his helmet, like bat to baseball, at top velocity. *Bam*. I felt the explosion in my wrist. That's what it felt like: like everything inside my wrist had just blown up. I knew this wasn't good. It hurt like hell. My right hand felt like it had instantly frozen over.

"You okay?" the team doc asked as I came off the field, sort of cradling my right arm, which was now a dangling appendage: no strength, no feeling. "Doc, I don't know what's going on, but this hand, I can't feel it, it's frozen," I said, making a beeline for one of the massive heaters on the sideline. I put both hands in front of the hot air. No dice. My left hand felt like it was on fire, but the right was still frozen solid.

They took me to the locker room for X-rays. Apparently, I'd dislocated the lunate bone, part of which popped out, flipped over, and was pressing on an artery, pinching the blood flow. At the hospital, a bunch of folks had to hold me down while the doctor tried to re-dislocate the bone and fit it back into the correct socket, to get it off that artery. No luck.

Can I just tell you? I think I have a high tolerance for pain, but this was at a level I'd never experienced. See, they can't put you under for this, because they need to hear from you whether feeling is coming back into the hand. So there I lay, held down, while a doc put his knee into my elbow for leverage and started to, in effect, re-dislocate my wrist. Over and over again. After ten tries, it was time to rush me into surgery, where the doctor explained to me what had happened.

"Look, this is a really bad injury," he said. "When that bone came out, it tore every ligament in your wrist, and those ligaments went into that socket where the bone had been. So no matter what, there wasn't room for that bone to get back into its socket. What they were trying to do in the ER was like trying to force something into a solid hole."

Uh, kinda woulda been nice to know before being tortured. The effects of that pain in the ER stayed with me for months. I'd walk down the steps, clutching the handrail, going a step at a time, just because I was so fearful of reinjuring the wrist and having to withstand that pain again. For months, I'd think about it, and cry and shake. Anni said I was having a post-traumatic stress reaction.

The recovery was a bitch. In not one, not two, but *three* wrist surgeries, docs had to put a total of five pins inside my wrist to hold all my junk together. For months, the pain was excruciating. I've never been a pill popper, but for about two months the only way I could get through the pain in order to grab three hours of sleep was to down three Percocets and two shots of vodka. I would go from pain to plastered in like three seconds, and then the pain would wake me in a few hours.

At home, I had a lot of hours to consider all that had gone down. I'd tied the franchise record for consecutive games but didn't break it. Friends seemed more bummed about that than I did. I felt that it was pretty cool to be tied with Harold Carmichael, a class act. And it felt small to sit around and feel sorry for myself for not breaking a record. The accomplishment is in the doing, and I played 162 straight NFL games. I just couldn't feel bummed. Mostly, my wrist in a cast and Percocets ever at the ready, I still felt really, really lucky.

Meantime, I had two comebacks to consider: magic and football. It took six months before I was able to shuffle a deck of cards. But football? Hell, I was thirty-six years old. A part of me said to myself: *It's been a helluva run. Walk away.*

But another part of me thought, *Screw that. Go out on your terms.*

• • •

It's a favorite topic on sports radio, in the newspapers, and on Twitter: *So-and-so's knees are shot. He should retire.* It's a part of the daily sports story, right? The wily veteran who should hang up his cleats, or the bust of a draft pick who should get a real job. But when you take a step back, it's kind of weird, isn't it? Athletes retire at an age when the rest of the world is just getting settled into adulthood. In what other industry are there public calls for you to "retire" when you're in your thirties?

In the spring of 2017, as I looked hard at retiring from the game, it dawned on me just how rare my situation was. I had another flourishing career, and I'd spent a lifetime training myself to define myself not by what I do but by how I approach life. A lot of the guys I played with never had that luxury. As a result, we've created generations of ex-jocks who, when the cheering stops, struggle to adjust to civilian life.

The statistics are staggering. Seventy percent of NFL players go bankrupt or experience financial distress within two years of retirement. The same fate awaits 60 percent of NBA players within five years. Divorce rates for retired athletes range upward of 60 percent. The depression rate of retired NFL players is 11 percent, according to one study.

Obviously, a lot of factors contribute to pro-athlete retirement issues. But the one I keep coming back to is what tennis great Andre Agassi was talking about when he observed that "professional sports can keep people from becoming who they really are." I saw it time and again in fourteen years of NFL locker rooms: there are guys who think that what they *do* is who they *are*. So, when the thing they've spent their lives doing is over, who are they?

When former Packers offensive lineman Tom Neville, unemployed and depressed, was shot and killed in a standoff with police three years after his 1995 retirement, his fellow offensive lineman Ken Ruettgers phoned many of their former teammates so they could all talk together, for the first time, about the challenges of transition. Ruettgers found widespread depression and a lot of lost souls, and he could relate—even though he'd earned an MBA while in the NFL.

"When so much of your self-worth is tied up with what you did, then who are you?" Ruettgers once told *Sports Illustrated*. So he founded Game's Over, a nonprofit that helps athletes adjust to life away from the game. And he found that, overwhelmingly, athletes suffer from "identity foreclosure": they see themselves as athletes to the exclusion of all other roles, such as father, husband, or businessman. It's common to all type A personalities: the job and the individual become one. And when the job is gone, so is the story you tell yourself and others about who you are.

So I had to ask myself: If I kept playing, was it because my story was dependent upon me being an NFL player?

In the end, after a lot of self-interrogation, I decided I could live without the game. I had Anni and I had my fifty-two buddies. What more could I need for a joyous, loving life? And yet . . . I decided to go for it. To come back and play again. Why?

I loved the game, but even more than the game, I loved the camaraderie that came with it. Just hanging in the locker room with my bros. Laughing our asses off. Did I *need* that? No. But it sure was cool to walk into that locker room, see my boys, and feel the safety of family.

Then there was the outpouring of love I felt from the fans after my injury. I saved every voice mail, text message, and get-well card I received. Media talks shit all the time about Philly sports fans, but let me tell you: it's all BS. There's no fan base that's more loving and sentimental. Big, burly, beer-drinking guys will throw their arms around you and tell you they love you. And they'll hug you like you're a long-lost bro home for the holidays. A part of me couldn't quit those crazy bastards.

Finally, I couldn't stop thinking about one thing that *was* missing: a Super Bowl. I *could* live without it, but it sure would be cool to go to one. And that meant I couldn't stop thinking about Carson Wentz. You get to Super Bowls with guys like him.

So, gingerly at first, I started snapping. And that's when I discovered the damnedest thing. Due to my now permanent lack of range of motion, I couldn't follow through on my snaps like I used to. That follow-through, if it got too pronounced, would put a little tail on the end of my ball in its flight, so it would break away from our punter, Donnie Jones. You couldn't see it with the naked eye, but I'd feel it and Donnie would know when it happened. At most, when it did, it cost him a millisecond to make the adjustment in order to catch it. Soon that tail was gone. Every snap was dead center. Could this be real? Could I really be snapping *better* after surgery?

I called the Eagles and told them I'd stumbled onto an entrepreneurial opportunity. I'd start a snapping camp with a unique pitch: "Line up, kids. I'm going to smash your wrist with a baseball bat. You'll come back in eight months to thank me."

I was officially on the comeback trail.

CHAPTER FOURTEEN

New Beginnings

Even if you're on the right track, you'll get run over if you just sit there.

—Will Rogers

"It took you fifteen years to figure this shit out," Donnie Jones said, laughing. We were on the field during training camp, and I'd just been snapping to him, each missile just as precise as the one before, each a tight, crisp spiral arriving to him—a left-footed punter—aligned with his left hip, his ideal kicking location. "You're like a friggin' machine!"

"I'm telling you, it's the wrist," I said. "It's all the surgeries." We laughed, shaking our heads in wonder. Life sure is weird sometimes. I'd been snapping for just about my whole adult life, and this was first time I actually felt like I'd totally *mastered* it, particularly on punts. In the past, when I'd struggled, it was because my punt snaps might have "ears" on them—a slight flutter. But now, no matter what else might happen on the field, I could repeat the same snap over and over, all external pressures be damned.

I was splitting the number of snaps with Rick Lovato, the twenty-four-year-old who had replaced me for the three games after my wrist blew up at the end of the previous season. Rick's a

helluva good kid with some real talent. He reminds me of someone: he busts his ass. Youth being what it is, I could tell he hadn't
yet figured out all the mental parts of the game. He was still
checking out what was being said about him on Twitter and listening to sports-talk radio in the morning; I'd seen teammates—
grown-ass men—who'd let sports yakkers' on-air whining about
them totally destroy their confidence.

Are you kidding me right now? I wanted to say to them. Those
radio guys are about sixty years old and haven't ever thrown a ball
on any kind of field. And you're letting *them* inside your head?
They're entertainers. Your job—and I said this to Rick—is to
freeze that stuff out. But some things take time, and he'd come to
that realization on his own—just like I did.

Despite splitting the snaps with Rick, I was feeling very much
like a thirty-seven-year-old. After each play, I'd return to the sideline, out of breath and just beat. "Man, I'm even more of an unathletic white dude now," I told Anni.

The fatigue felt new. Maybe all the off-season surgeries depleted
some of my energy reserves. My body had been through some
trauma—it was unrealistic to expect it to perform like it had before
the injury, right? So each day, I took my snaps and threw myself
into punt coverage, just waiting for the old feeling to return.

I had less time than I knew. The day after we'd beaten the
Miami Dolphins 38–31 in our third preseason game, I was sitting
at my locker when special-teams coach Dave Fipp came in and sat
down next to me. He leaned forward. "Jon," he said, "I'm going
to go with the younger guy."

Now, in most industries, you can't say that to an employee;
football, however, ain't one of them. There's no such thing as age
discrimination. Old athletes fade away—it's the natural order of
things. Still, I was stunned.

"I appreciate your honesty," I said.

Fipp shifted uncomfortably. "What would you do if you weren't here?" he asked.

"Hmm," I said. "Well, there are only two options. I'll go play somewhere else or retire, I guess."

This, I knew, was key information for the Eagles. If I wanted to keep playing, they'd try to trade me. But first they'd need to know that I'd report to wherever they sent me. Of course, the notion of trading me sounded crazy: I was a long snapper, for crying out loud. We don't get traded. We get cut, and then, if we're lucky, we get signed.

Wow. Just like that, eleven years in Philly—done. It was hard to wrap my head around the idea. At first, all the predictable thoughts came. I'd gone through all those surgeries in the off-season, all that pain. For *this*? Intellectually, I knew what I was doing: I was spinning my own victim narrative. Nevertheless, I started to wonder: What was this *really* about? Did my coaches resent that my whole life didn't revolve around football, and that I'd been outspoken about how unhealthy it is when football blots out all else in life? That, when asked, I'd been vocal about how many men in the game desperately needed to find balance in their lives? Could that be a part of it?

I flashed back on a team event in which my teammate Donnie Jones and I found ourselves chatting with the spouse of one of our coaches. The coach wasn't there—he was back in the team facility, where he'd been around-the-clock, going so far as to sleep on an air mattress in his office. Donnie texted him: "Hey, with your wife here—come over!" The coach texted right back: "Can't—working on game plan. Have fun." What stuck with me in this moment was his wife's reaction to the text: "He didn't return *my* texts," she said.

I was saddened by that, and a little outraged. *Dude*, I wanted to say, *you'd actually be a better coach if you spent more time with your wife and kids.* Players want to play for guys who are loving, and not fearful or insecure. Now here I was, literally told I was no longer part of the team. Was it because my values differed so much from those calling the shots inside our building? Did they actually resent my magic? My local TV show? The fact that I was stalking Kevin James on the sideline, or that I was out and about, mingling with fans every chance I got, rather than holed up watching videotape of our opponents all night long?

The truth is, I was overthinking it—which is what happens when you get a blow to the ego. It probably wasn't near as complicated as I was making it: I was thirty-seven years old, and the Eagles could save $825,000 on the salary cap by getting rid of my tired ass. But getting cut or traded plays with your mind.

I'd seen it. A lot of athletes have been told they're the shit since their early teens. They've risen to the top of their profession. And when a team cuts or trades them, it's like they're suddenly in junior high and a girl has dumped them for the first time. It's the first time you've been told you're not wanted. It unleashes a tsunami of emotional stuff.

Fans think of players as supermen or stats for their fantasy lineups, but we're flesh and blood, with the same hang-ups and frailties as everybody else. We're just in a very public, very cutthroat business. But that doesn't mean we don't feel.

A few summers ago, a video went viral on social media when it was reported during a game that New York Met Wilmer Flores had been traded. Well, there he was—on the field, in his Mets uniform, when the news broke, and, in front of thousands of fans and many more watching on TV, my man just started bawling his eyes out. The trade ultimately didn't go through, but Flores had to sweat it out for a few hours while fans gave him a total of four standing ovations. Once the team announced the deal wouldn't happen, two days later Flores belted an extra-innings walk-off home run.

You gotta love that story, but what stayed with me was just how emotional Flores got. "I was sad," he later said. "Being a Met forever, I have all my teammates here, that's why I got emotional." Hear, hear, Wilmer. My team was my family. How could I not be sad at the thought of being separated from them?

Look, I'm not complaining. I'm the first to admit how lucky I've been, and to acknowledge that athletes tend to be a pretty transient bunch. My friends in the NBA call it a "renter's league," because most teams are built to feature two or three star players who will be there a long time, and most of their teammates will change from year to year.

But let's not pretend that it's "just business" and doesn't leave emotional scars. Or that it's not stressful. Think about how much it sucks to move just a couple of towns over. You've got to pack, hire movers, and then wait around for a day or two for the damned cable guy. Research has found that moving can be as stressful as going through a divorce. Well, now imagine you've got to move in a matter of hours—throw some stuff in a bag, hop a flight, and meet your new team within hours, maybe clear across the country. I've seen guys get traded and bolt for the locker room door like they're a fugitive on the run.

That I was with one team for eleven seasons made me one lucky dude. How'd you like to have been Bobo Newsom, the most traded man in baseball history? He was sold or traded *fourteen* times before he retired in 1953. "I played for Washington five different times," Newsom famously once said. "That beat Franklin Delano Roosevelt's record. He was only elected four times."

Then there was Mike Sillinger, the most traded man in hockey history. He played for twelve different teams and was traded nine times in his career. Of the twelve clubs he played for, he spent a whole season with only four of them. It was a nomadic life; his wife used to visit just to do his laundry.

People just don't like change. But by now, I knew that change could be my friend. Within a day, I was starting to come to terms with the end of my time as an Eagle. After Fipp broke the news to me, general manager Howie Roseman asked if I'd be interested in playing for the Jacksonville Jaguars. Eh, not so much. Chicago? Too cold. But then he was back: the New Orleans Saints were offering a seventh-round pick next season for me.

Now we were talking. "Hell, yes," I said. I kid you not—my first thought was: *The Saints are Ellen's favorite team. How cool is that?* She grew up in Louisiana, and was a huge fan of Saints quarterback Drew Brees. I started thinking about the three of us hanging out together, especially when she tweeted, tagging the Saints when the news broke: "Your team just added a whole lotta magic."

There was also this: I'd get to play more than half my games in a dome. No more crappy weather. Instead of fearing change, suddenly I was starting to get excited. New Orleans was a cool town, with great music and food, and it was a whole new fan base for me to tap into. I asked Roseman if any long snapper had ever been traded for a draft pick. "I don't think so," he said. How about that? Maybe I was making history. Now, not only was I getting into it, but the whole deal *really* made sense from the Eagles' point of view: They were getting a draft pick for a thirty-seven-year-old who was coming off an injury. Kind of a no-brainer, huh?

For me, it was off to N'awlins, but not before feeling a whole lotta love from the Philly fans and my teammates. Sports-radio phone lines lit up with fans complaining that I'd been traded. A part of me was tempted to call in and say, *Yo, this makes total sense for the Eagles. Rick is more than ready to step up, and I'm off to create new memories somewhere else.*

That's also what I told my teammates, many of whom were concerned about what my absence would mean for locker room chemistry. Publicly, Jeffrey Lurie released a beautiful statement to the press once the news broke.

"Jon is one of the most inspiring people I have ever known," he said. "He gave everything that he had to this organization for more than a decade, but his legacy in Philadelphia goes far beyond his performance on the field, his Pro Bowl selections or the consecutive-games streak. His true impact is measured by the number of people in this city that he connected with, the lives he has been able to change and the courage he displays every day after battling such tremendous adversity as a child."

He was just as gracious when, before releasing his public statement, he called me on my cell. "This is the hardest part of this game," Jeff said. "You know, Jon, if you want to stay, play one more year, and then retire as an Eagle, I'll make that happen."

Wow. Instinctively, I knew that if I took him up on such a kind offer, it would be because the competitor in me wanted to prove Coach Fipp wrong. It would be my ego talking. "I love you, man," I said. "You know what? It's all good. If it's my time, let it be. If Coach Fipp doesn't want me around, I don't want to be here. Let's shake hands and go on our way."

"Coach Fipp was adamant about making a change, and I've got to trust him," Jeff said. "But you'll always be an Eagle. You'll always be family."

"It's all good, Jeff," I said. "I never thought I'd take a snap in the NFL. You've given me a home for eleven years. Man, I'd die for you."

And with that, it was time to move on. I didn't do any media, and I said good-bye to only a few special people: Donnie Jones, Big Dom, equipment operations manager Greg Delimitros, team president Don Smolenski, and CFO Frank Gumienny. I'd spent eleven years with the Eagles and had made countless friends for life on the team. But I didn't want to make this all about me and I didn't want to focus on the past. The Saints wanted me, so I bolted to get to New Orleans.

While I was en route—Anni would meet me there—my teammates showed me some love in the media. "His positive attitude is something that's hard to find in a football locker room all year round," safety Malcolm Jenkins was quoted as saying. "Jon's the guy who is constantly in a good mood, constantly joking around. He's just a good friend and obviously a guy who is going to be missed."

Rick Lovato handled it beautifully—I was proud of him: "I'm not trying to fill his shoes," he said. "There's no taking anything away from him. I just want to do my job, keep my head down, not try to be noticeable."

Once I touched down in New Orleans, I started hearing from my Eagle teammates. Apparently, some of them were upset enough by the trade that Coach Fipp felt compelled to make a presentation to the team explaining his thinking as to why it was time to move on from me; one angry teammate told me it felt like I'd been kicked in the ass on my way out.

I just repeated what I'd said to Jeff. "It's all good, man," I said.

Sensitivities were high; a couple of weeks before, the team had traded veteran wide receiver Jordan Matthews to Buffalo. Jordan was a cool dude and had become great friends with Carson Wentz. When two loud voices are removed from a locker room—even when change makes sense from a football perspective—it can wreak havoc with team chemistry. Doug Pederson was an emotionally intelligent coach, though. "It can definitely affect the team," he said, when asked about me and Jordan leaving. "Guys really respected these guys and liked them. And now they can influence another locker room, and they can take what they've learned here to another organization, another franchise. I wish both of those guys well. But it can affect guys, but it only affects you if you let it. That's my job, not to let that happen."

Dougie would figure that out. Me? I was already living it up in the Big Easy.

• • •

There must have been thirty of them when I walked into the locker room—my new teammates, waiting at my locker. What a greeting. Brees, running back Mark Ingram, and defensive back Obum Gwacham were among them. "Magic man!" someone called out.

"Let's see a trick!" someone else yelled.

And we were off. I wowed them with some sleight of hand then and there, while guys started streaming in to see the show. Phones were whipped out and posts found their way to YouTube. At one point, I opened my mouth wide and, while guys screamed and high-fived one another, a deck of cards came flowing out from it.

Man, what a welcome. You couldn't have scripted anything better. The reality is, change is good. I felt a surge of energy running through my body. I was the new kid at school; I was gonna bring it. I was gonna prove to the Saints that they'd done the right thing betting on me.

Within seconds of entering the Saints training facility, I felt not only welcomed but also needed; the Saints had a hole at long snapper. In the last few weeks, they'd released two snappers, which meant the job belonged to Justin Drescher. But after the team's most recent preseason game, Justin was on the sideline in a boot with a foot injury. They decided they had to move on from him when I became available. "You're gonna love this city and this organization," Justin, who would catch on with the Arizona Cardinals, told me when I reached out just before rolling into town.

As if I needed a sign that this was where I was meant to be, it turned out that I had a history with special-teams coach Brad Banta. He was a tight end and long snapper who'd had ten seasons in the league and had been hoping for an eleventh in 2004—when I tore my ACL as a Bill in Week 13. Brad was at home, painting his house, and had just told his wife that it looked like his career was over . . . when the Bills called, looking to pick him up as my replacement for the last three games of the season. Turns out, you need to play in at least three games to be credited for a year of service. Now, seeing me in the New Orleans locker room after all this time, Brad threw his arms around me. "You gave me eleven," he said. "Now I'm gonna give you fifteen."

At practice, a group of reporters wanted to know what I was feeling. I talked about how cool it was to be wanted, and that I'd always wanted to play in New Orleans. My Eagle teammates Malcolm Jenkins and Darren Sproles, who'd both starred for the Saints, had told me I'd love the city. Plus, I'd been friends with Saints punter Thomas Morstead for years, so I was stoked to work with him. One of the reporters asked why I'd always wanted to play here.

"One, the city," I said. "Two, who's not a Drew Brees fan? So, to play with him, and the tradition. In the off-season, you would talk to guys who have come through here, and it was, like, 'Dude, Coach [Sean] Payton is awesome, the organization is awesome.' And just the camaraderie, it leaks throughout the league."

Meantime, Coach Payton was telling the press I'd play in this week's preseason game against Baltimore, and that I had solved their snapping woes. When asked what he liked about me, the coach replied: "His consistency. He's a veteran player. There's a presence about him. He's done it over a long time."

At practice, I felt myself falling in love with football all over again. The vibe was positive and Brees was the type of leader you'd want to follow to the ends of the earth. He's not the loudest guy in the room and he doesn't get up in your grill. Instead, he gives off a quiet selflessness.

You ever see that Jerry Seinfeld routine about how crazy our sports addiction is? "Loyalty to any one sports team is pretty hard to justify," he says. "Because the players are always changing, the team can move to another city. You're actually rooting for the clothes when you get right down to it. You are standing and cheering and yelling for your clothes to beat the clothes from another city. Fans will be so in love with a player but if he goes to another team, they boo him. This is the same human being in a different shirt, they *hate* him now. *Boo!*, different shirt! *Boo!*"

That always cracked me up. But Drew was the exception to Seinfeld's rule, just like I'd been in Philly. You couldn't say I wasn't from Philly during my time there, just like you can't say Drew isn't a vital part of New Orleans. He first came to the city in 2006, after being cut by the San Diego Chargers. He had a bum shoulder and wasn't sure he'd have any takers on the open market. But the Saints took him in, just after Katrina.

"I had no place to go, no place to call home, and wasn't sure if I was going to play football again," Brees recalled. "Here came New Orleans, six months post-Katrina, with a new head coach, and really in the same situation I was. Trying to resurrect a career, and the city. I felt like it was a true calling for my wife and [me] to come to New Orleans and be a part of the resurgence of a team, but more importantly, of a city and a community. And the passion and resiliency of the people of New Orleans is something that continues to keep us going every day."

How can you not love this guy? He not only brought New Orleans the Super Bowl in 2010, but also, off the field, his foundation raised more than $25 million for Katrina relief. The best leaders, I've learned, lead by doing, and their example makes you want to do better. I couldn't wait to get to practice because of the passion and commitment that Drew Brees gave off.

Then again, the whole city was inspiring. After our final pre-season game—man, it felt good to be out there—the city opened itself to us. Out at dinner, strangers would approach. "We're so glad you're here," they'd say. In Philly, strangers would high-five or burst into a vein-popping rendition of the Eagles fight song,

"Fly, Eagles, Fly." Here, it was less testosterone-fueled, usually a quick welcome or a pat on the back.

Anni and I played house at the Hilton while we looked for rentals. We found a kick-ass spot downtown in a high-rise with an amazing view from our twenty-by-forty-foot deck. I'd spent all this time in the Northeast; now I'd be able to sit out on our patio well into November, grilling up some steaks and watching the love of my life sip a glass of wine. Until now, we'd lived in my South Philly condo—the one I'd shared with my ex-wife. This spot would be *ours*.

I felt ten years younger. How silly it was for me to have been bummed about moving on from the Eagles, whose GM, Howie Roseman, sent me a note, wishing me well and asking if I was "sure I was done being an Eagle." Uh, I appreciate the love, but *you* traded *me*, bro.

But it was all good. I was all in as a Saint. One night, as my fifteenth regular season was about to begin, Anni and I sat out on our deck and shared a bottle of vino. "It doesn't get any better than this," I said, clinking our glasses.

In the morning, she'd be heading back to Philly, where she'd meet with the movers and get all our stuff shipped to New Orleans. Before practice, I'd be completing the second half of my physical, which is mandated by the NFL upon any trade. But I'd already played one game as a Saint, so this would just be a formality.

Afterward, I wanted to think some more about how to take this town by storm. "Hey," I said to Anni now, "do you know if Mardi Gras has a commissioner? I want to be the commissioner of Mardi Gras." She laughed, seeing the wheels starting to turn. Hey, why not? In Philly, I had been the commissioner of the legendary Wing Bowl, which each year drew more than twenty thousand rabid fans at dawn to cheer on their favorite professional eaters. Anni and I clinked our glasses, toasting again to our good fortune.

CHAPTER FIFTEEN

Man Plans
and God Laughs

I hope to arrive to my death late, in love, and a little drunk.
—Atticus

Thomas Morstead, our punter, saw the changing of my life go down in real time. He was in the locker room with me when my cell phone rang. It was a 504 area code—a local call. I'd been back for about an hour after undergoing a medical test at the hospital. Earlier in the day, our doc, John Amoss, an internal medicine specialist, had listened to my breathing with a stethoscope and didn't like what he heard. So much for the mere formality of a physical.

I could tell something didn't sit right with him. Just to be safe, he said, he was sending me to the hospital for an echocardiogram—a test that checks how your heart's chambers and valves are pumping blood. I'm all for being precautionary. "Let's roll," I said.

Well, now, back in the locker room, this local call must have been my green light. Only, *not*. As I listened to the voice on the other end of the call, Morstead would later say he saw my jaw drop, and knew instantly something was wrong. "It was scary," he said.

It was the cardiologist Dr. Amoss had sent me to. "I don't know how to put this, but these results, these were not what we were thinking or what we were hoping for," he said. "I don't know how to say this, other than to tell you you're never going to play football again and we need to have you back here right away for more tests. We'll call the coach and get it all squared away, but you need to know this is pretty serious."

Hearing those words, it would strike me later, was like hearing "There was an accident and your mom didn't make it" when I was twelve. You hear the words in plain English, but you don't *understand* them, not really. It's like you suddenly don't speak the language. Later, I'd reflect on how a person's life can change in a nanosecond. One instant, you're a professional athlete; the next, you're in a fight for your very life. One instant, you're a carefree twelve-year-old at baseball camp; the next, your mom is dead, your dad is under arrest, and you're essentially orphaned.

None of this struck me as Morstead watched me try to process this information. I was too busy being stunned. Waves of adrenaline kicked in; all I could hear was the loud beating of my own heart. I don't remember if Morstead and I even spoke. He watched me wander out of the locker room and into the training room.

There, I sat across from head athletic trainer Scottie Patton and director of sports medicine Beau Lowery. They got the cardiologist on speakerphone. That's when I first heard the term "aortic aneurysm," a weakened area in the upper part of the aorta, which is the major blood vessel feeding blood to the body. An aneurysm can lead to a tear in the arterial wall that can lead to life-threatening bleeding.

I was still reeling as I made my way upstairs, to Coach Sean Payton's office. It's funny, the questions that first come to your mind. "Coach, should I wait to call my wife?" I asked. "She's back in Philly, making the move happen. The tests I'm about to have, are they to gather more information about what this might be, or is it just to double-check? If we don't know one hundred percent what this is, should I wait to call her until we really know what's going on?"

You know what that is? *Denial.* I was looking for an escape hatch. *We're getting more tests done. Maybe this isn't all that bad.* Coach Payton, God bless him, knew what I was up to, even if I didn't.

"No, the cardiologist says you're done," he said. "This is a serious problem. Call your wife. This is happening, Jon."

This is happening, Jon. That was just what I needed: a verbal head slap. Coach Payton called the doctor. "Coach, not to put too fine a point on it," the doc said on speakerphone, "but if we didn't catch this and Jon were to play Monday night, there's a better than fifty-fifty chance he'd have died on the field, before the ambulance could get him to me. One shot to the sternum, and this thing will rupture."

Oh. My. God. It hit me: feet, meet edge of cliff. Sitting across from Coach Payton, I called Anni. The movers were scheduled to be at the condo in the morning—everything was out of the cabinets and ready to be packed up. She was in an Uber, heading to yoga.

Do I let her go to yoga and just breathe a little before hitting her with all this? Hmm. There was no way in hell that telling her in a couple of hours that I was in the hospital undergoing tests could possibly fly. No, better to dive in.

"Anni, I don't know how to tell you this," I said. "During the physical, they discovered something. I'm done playing football and I need emergency heart surgery. I'm on my way to the hospital now for more tests. I'm okay, but we need more information."

"*What* did you tell me?" she shrieked. Without missing a beat, she ordered the Uber driver to turn around. He'd take her home to grab a few things and then on to the airport. She was on her way.

Meantime, I underwent another echocardiogram and a CT test with dye. Turns out, my condition had zero to do with diet or behavior. I was born with a congenital heart defect known as a bicuspid aortic valve, the valve that transports blood flow from the heart. It's an inherited form of heart disease in which two of the leaflets of the valve fuse together in the womb. It is the most common cause of heart disease present at birth and affects between 1 and 2 percent of adults.

The walls of the aorta are typically strong enough to tolerate the stress of blood flow from the heart. Aneurysms—which develop in about half of all patients with bicuspid valves—occur when the walls weaken. As the weakened wall deteriorates, it leaves behind damaged tissue that grows in size, heightening the risk of a serious tear.

The aortic valve is supposed to be three centimeters. Mine? The size of a can of Coca-Cola. So *that's* why time was of the essence.

"Did you ever have any symptoms?" the doctor asked.

"What's a symptom?"

"Ever been out of breath?"

"Doc," I said. "I'm a slow white guy. I was surrounded by these freaks of nature. I was *always* out of breath. I always had to work twice as hard just to keep up."

"I can't tell you for how long, but you've been working really inefficiently, Jon," he said. "As you've been running, you've been losing blood—it's been going back into the heart. So your body has had to work two or three times as hard just to maintain, let alone excel."

Now the fatigue from training camp was starting to make sense. Or that time during our honeymoon, when Anni and I went swimming with sharks. She was underwater with them, but I couldn't hold my breath for more than a few seconds before having to come up, gasping for air. "Man," I remember saying, "I'm more out of shape than I thought."

Until a few hours ago, I was a professional athlete. Now I was being told I need emergency open-heart surgery to repair or replace the valve and remove the aneurysm—and I need it within the next few days. How serious was this? Turns out, it was the same condition that killed Alan Thicke and John Ritter, and actor Bill Paxton died of a postsurgical complication from this very condition.

Meantime, the slightest movement could trigger an eruption. Don't lift anything over five pounds. Don't run. Don't raise your voice. Don't have caffeine. Don't have sex. Just sit there. Find a surgeon and have this done. "If you were to play and got hit hard and your heart decided to take a couple of extra pumps," the doc said, "that could cause a rupture."

Well, hello, new life. Leaving the hospital, I'd just been told my life was in danger. Anni was on her way, but not with me yet. I was tempted to feel all alone and go to a really dark place. I could feel that familiar "why me?" narrative bubbling up.

But then, hitting the down button at the elevator bank, I saw it, sitting there, looking up at me from the most pristine floor you could imagine. A shiny, single penny. I had to smile.

Whenever they'd see a penny, Nonnie and Susan always said, it would make them think of Mom. So ever since I was a kid, I'd throw pennies onto sidewalks or streets in the hope that Nonnie or Susan or anyone who believed in pennies from heaven would find them. It was a way to keep Mom with us. As an adult, I continued to throw a penny whenever I got one, a silent kiss to Mom. So would Anni. So would my man Tim Mooney.

If you'd lived my life, you'd believe in signs, too, bro. Don't tell me *that* penny on *that* floor at *that* time wasn't a sign. How *could* I feel alone? Mom was with me.

The next five days were a blur. The Eagles and Saints worked out the football stuff. Even though I played a preseason game for the

Saints, my heart condition meant that I'd technically failed my physical, so the trade had to be rescinded. My heart condition was a preexisting condition. That meant my whole contract—three years, $3.4 million—was null and void. It's like I didn't even know it, but I'd gone to the casino and, in one instant, blown millions.

And you know what? I couldn't care less. There's nothing that refocuses the mind, and reminds you of your priorities, like a life-or-death battle. And that's what this was. It didn't take me long to realize that in a way, I'd been preparing for this moment my whole life. Ever since I was twelve years old, I'd been learning how to discard distractions and just focus on the task at hand.

There was no time for panic or worry or fear. We needed a game plan. "We're going to attack this like I've done my entire life," I told Anni, which was easier said than done.

Particularly for Anni. We'd been married for just shy of three months. Life hadn't just thrown her a curve ball, it had dropped a meteor on her. A couple of times, we both suffered panic attacks, dropping to the floor in our kitchen, shaking and hyperventilating. But I'd never felt so loved and cared for. She was with me every step of the way; we were there for each other. "We've got to get it together," I said. "Because we're going to get through this. We'll be fine. Let's find a surgeon, get in, get out. Let's do what we do."

I'm afraid I turned pretty ice-cold about it. Rather than process any of the events that were happening, I was just dead focused. I'm not sure it even really dawned on me that in a matter of days, I'd be having open-heart surgery. All I could think about was what was right in front of me: we're going to find the best surgeon and medical team in the world, we're going to have them do what they do, and this will go down in the next few days.

Nothing else mattered, except breathing and staying alive. I had to make out a will, but it was all a formality. I signed papers but didn't read them. "Babe," I told Anni, "this ain't the game plan. The game plan is, we're going to beat this and survive."

Here's what's great about Anni and me; actually, it's what's great about any loving relationship. We took turns picking each other up. When she felt panic, I was there to snap her out of it. And when she sensed that *I* was steering toward fear or doubt, she brought me back. "We're going to get through this by talking to ourselves and not listening to ourselves," she told me, quoting me to me, bringing me back from whatever nervousness I might have been feeling.

We started doing our due diligence. Between Google and the recommendations of the Saints, the Eagles, and a few friends, we compiled a list of surgeons. I was blown away by how many texts I received from throughout the NFL with doctor references and get-well wishes. Opposing coaches who I never thought even liked me reached out—like Coach Tom Quinn, the New York Giants specials-teams coach who kept his eye on me back when I played with those torn ligaments in my ankle under Coach Reid. "I loved playing against you," Coach Quinn texted. "You're a great competitor. I always knew that when we played you we would have to play our best. The game will miss you. If one of my guys had what you have, here's the doc we'd send them to."

Anni and I spoke on the phone to docs in Houston, Alabama, Los Angeles, and Cleveland. All sounded great. But in all these conversations, the name of *another* doc kept popping up. He had taught many of them the exact procedure I now needed. And it turns out, this badass regularly traveled the globe to teach others how to repair aortic valves and snuff out aneurysms. The best part? He was a Philly guy. Joe Bavaria was at the University of Pennsylvania, and, it turned out, he'd long been known globally as the father of this very surgery. The better-than-best part? Dude's an Eagles fan.

When we got him on the phone, there were no pleasantries, there was no chitchat. He got right to the point. "Dorenbos," he said, "I heard about this. I can't tell you how excited I am that you called me. I'm just going to lay it out there for you. There's nobody better than me at this. I'm going to tell you right now, if you were just having a valve replacement, yeah, there are a handful of surgeons in America you could go to, and you'd be fine. But if you want a valve replacement and an aneurysm fix? Get your ass on a plane, come to Philly, and let me save your life."

I looked at Anni, and we both were tearing up. We'd found our man. "What's the difference between God and a doctor?" an old joke asks. "God knows he's not a doctor." Well, Bavaria carries himself with what some might think of as a God complex. But I think of it as swagger, which is exactly what you want from a guy into whose hands you're placing your life. Brian Dawkins's alter ego needed its own locker? Damn straight. Because if you want to be that good at something, you don't just study it. You become it. You want to be Dr. Bavaria? You become the baddest muthafucka with a stethoscope on the planet. You carry yourself with confidence, and others will have confidence in you.

I'm in, I told Bavaria. We quickly packed and were Philly bound. How to get there? Jeffrey Lurie already had that taken care of it. He'd called me as soon as the news broke about my condition. "Listen, Jon, you've got the use of my plane," he said. "You have to go to Germany to get this taken care of? I've got you. Just say the word and it will take you anywhere in the world."

"Well, actually, it's going to be a lot more convenient than going to Germany," I told Jeff now. We were headed back to Philly.

Thanks to Jeff, Anni and I were soon sitting across from Dr. Bavaria in his office at the University of Pennsylvania. To look at him, you wouldn't think he was a superhero. He was tall, normal build, graying hair, sandy beard. More likely to be a familiar face at the farmers' market or at the dog park. But that's just it: extraordinary people come in ordinary packages every day.

I asked Bavaria, simply, *Why?* After all, he's not only a cardiac surgeon, but *the* guy for bicuspid aortic valves and aneurysms. How does someone get to be the best in the world at *that?*

He laughed. "How does someone become an NFL long snapper *and* a magician?" he said. Turns out, he put in considerably more than his ten thousand hours, having performed more than six thousand open-heart surgeries, some four thousand of which were cardiac-valve related. Bavaria went to medical school after studying chemical engineering. An early mentor—*his* Ken Sands, if you will—was a cardiac surgeon.

"I thought it would be cool to be a heart surgeon," he said. That's when he noticed that mitral valves were being replaced all the time, but this procedure—aortic-valve replacement—wasn't being done with any regularity. "I knew that was going to be my niche," he said. "The world of the heart that nobody had really explored yet—that was going to be mine. So now I'm *the* guy, I do more of these than anybody, and I know more than anybody when it comes to exactly what you need."

Field general that he is, Bavaria walked us through his game plan. "The number one goal is to repair your existing valve," he said. "This is what I do. I'm an artist. It's a delicate, elegant operation."

If the valve couldn't be repaired and had instead to be replaced, Bavaria explained, he'd need us to make a choice before the surgery: Do we want a mechanical or a cadaver valve? If mechanical, I'd be on blood thinners for the rest of my life. If cadaver, we'd likely be back in another ten or fifteen years for more open-heart surgery, but I wouldn't be on any blood thinners. That sounded like the way for me: I could just go and *live* for a decade.

Once that was decided, into the hospital I went for a day of testing. And then it would be go time. How long would I be in surgery? About four hours, Bavaria said. Let's do this, I said.

Here's a word of advice: the night before you're undergoing emergency open-heart surgery, do not—I repeat, do *not*—Google your procedure. If you do, you'll see them literally sawing open a chest. It doesn't look like fun.

Susan had flown in, as had Krissy and Anni's mom, who'd been on a trip to Spain. Tim Mooney was there with us every step of the way. Susan was scheduled to leave in two days for Australia with two of her girlfriends—the trip of a lifetime. She wanted to cancel her plans, but I said no way. "You'll see that I'm okay after the surgery, and then you're going on that trip," I said.

We also had a surprise visitor: my brother, Randy, appeared out of nowhere in my hospital room. We'd drifted apart in recent years. I was touched he'd show up for me.

That night, I FaceTimed with my buddies and held Anni tight. Funny, it never even occurred to me to reach out to my dad. I'd been so focused on the game plan, all I could think about at the eleventh hour was touching base with the people who had been in my life all these years.

Come morning, that's when the fear hit. Anni and I were both crying when it was go time. She walked with me and held my hand as the orderlies wheeled me to the OR. Finally, we got to the end of a long hallway, which was as far as she could go with us. We kissed. Said "I love you." And then we rounded that corner; when I turned my head and could no longer see her . . . *that's* when I lost it. That was the worst feeling. Not seeing her. The fear and the dread, rising up in me.

Then, all of a sudden, the beeps got louder, the room got colder, and the ceiling got higher. I was in the OR. To my left, I noticed the saw and the scalpels and clamps. *This is happening, Jon.*

Now the anesthesiologist leaned over me. "Are you ready?" she asked.

"As ready as I'm ever going to be," I said. "Let's do this."

"Just tell me what island you want to go to, and you'll have a helluva vacation," she said.

She put the mask on me. I took it off. "I don't want to go to an island," I said, getting teary-eyed. "Take me back to my wedding day. The best day of my life. I don't tell my wife good-bye. I tell her, 'I'll kiss you soon.' That's where I want to go."

She touched my shoulder and I lowered the mask. The last thing I remember is closing my eyes and seeing myself dip my wife on the beach in Cabo.

What was supposed to be a four-hour surgery lasted more than ten. Bavaria would later say that my sternum was the hardest he'd ever had to crack. He had to stand on a stool to get enough leverage.

When he came out to speak to Anni, her heart dropped. Just imagine: she'd been waiting ten hours for a surgery that was supposed to last four, and now the doc approached—and he wasn't looking happy.

"I need to speak to Anni alone," he said to Susan, Krissy, and Tim Mooney. Mooney later told me he instantly thought: *Oh my God. Jon died on the table.*

What he didn't know was that Dr. Bavaria was just being compliant with hospital confidentiality laws. And that upset look on his face?

"I couldn't save the valve," Bavaria told Anni, beating himself up, like the true artist he is.

"Is Jon okay?" she blurted out.

"Oh, yeah, he's fine," the doc said. "But I couldn't repair that damned valve."

The anesthesiologist came out to walk Anni through what would be a slow return to consciousness. In a small percentage of cases, patients don't wake up. Annie would sit with me and talk to me and rejoice in small miracles, like when she felt me squeeze her hand after she'd asked me to. My girl pretty much lost it when the anesthesiologist told her that before going under, "Jon said he never tells you good-bye. He said he tells you he'll kiss you soon. Well, he'll be kissing you soon."

Slowly, I started to wake up, ever so groggily. Mooney made a crack about Eagles GM Howie Roseman saving my life—had he not traded me, my condition might not have been discovered. I don't remember, but there's some disagreement among those who were in the recovery room as to whether I raised a middle finger or a thumbs-up in response.

I'll never forget lying there, hooked up to the defibrillator machine. The nurses would put an ice chip on my lips every five minutes or so. Ice chips have never tasted so good. Private planes, the NFL, Ritz-Carlton suites . . . none of it mattered, or would matter ever again. I just remember biting those ice chips and holding Anni's hand. It's all that mattered. It was a strain to speak. "We alive, baby," I managed to say to Anni. It would become a common refrain between us.

CHAPTER SIXTEEN

The Comeback Kid

We make a living by what we get. We make a life by what we give.

—Winston Churchill

Dr. Bavaria warned us. When they go in and mess with your heart, the *emotional* fallout is . . . unpredictable. It can give rise to depression, irritability, anger. Nearly a quarter of patients who have gone through open-heart surgery experience some form of depression or mood swings. It makes sense, right? You've kinda had a broken heart. But Anni and I were, like, *yeah, right*. Me, depressed, irritable or angry? Me, Mr. Positivity?

Well, after the surgery, when it was time to take out the tubes that were hooked up to my chest in order to keep excess fluid from getting into my lungs, it was like a floodgate had been opened. As soon as the tubes were pulled from my body, I burst into tears. I'm talking *sobs*. Leading up to the surgery, I'd been so focused on the mission, I'd kept all this emotion in. Now here it came—in waves. And it would continue to come.

I became a blubbering, crying mess. Everything made me cry. I wasn't so much sad as . . . overwhelmed. I was so thankful, so humbled, just to be alive. A schmaltzy commercial on TV? Tears.

195

Anni's face while she peacefully slept next to my bed during my four weeks post-surgery in the hospital? Waterworks, again. The video that went viral on social media of a barroom full of Eagles fans chanting my name before the surgery? Oh, man, I almost couldn't take it. The outpouring of loving text messages? I'd break down each time my phone pinged, like one particular text after I'd posted this thought: "I was able to ride with the wind beneath my wings for 11 years only to have my life saved by a Saint." Ellen wrote in response: "You are a very special and brilliant man. I am so grateful to know you. I love you," and she sent a boxful of thirty DVDs—her favorite movies—for me to watch during my recovery.

We'd sit in that hospital room, Anni and I, and just look at each other and start to cry. "What the hell just happened?" I'd say as she hugged me.

"Can we not do that again, please?" she'd say.

The magnitude of what we'd been through was starting to hit me. And I do mean "we." Leading up to the surgery, I didn't think for a minute about how hard all this was on Anni. Now it dawned on me that she had it *worse* than I did—I'd rather go through it all again than have to wait more than ten hours for *her* to come out of lifesaving surgery.

I'd need physical *and* mental rehab to get back to being me. Putting one foot in front of the other while upright—walking, in other words—became a hurdle. The day after the surgery, I had to try it, to get the blood flowing and avoid clotting. Holding Anni's hand, I could make it—maybe—two or three shaky baby steps before I'd have to collapse, exhausted. When Donnie Jones came to visit, he went with me to physical therapy, in a room with a couple of steps, a three-pound dumbbell, and two patients hooked up to their IVs, sleeping. "You're shitting me, right?" Donnie said. "Last week, you were a pro athlete, and now *this* is your gym?"

As I got stronger, Anni and I would ever so slowly walk the halls of our floor. Each time she grabbed my hand, I'd look at our hands joined together and say, "This is my favorite part"; we'd both tear up, and then off we'd go. In short order, we'd turn these little excursions into a mission to change the culture of the floor. Because no one really talks to one another in the hospital. Every time we passed a fellow patient in the hallway or walked by a room with an open door, we'd be stared at. If we hadn't known any better, we'd've thought no one liked us.

But that wasn't it. Everybody was just so scared, man. No one knew what the hell to say to one another. I started thinking about Coach Reid. Once, when we were on a losing streak, I sat a couple of seats behind him on the team bus. "When the captain keeps his cool, the ship keeps its cool," I overheard him say. "If the captain loses his cool, the ship loses its cool."

Big Red always had a calmness about him—and it made his players comfortable in their own skin. *That's* what this floor needs, I told Anni. A leader to bring people together. Silver Ten—that was the name of our building—needed a coach.

So we started walking the floor and talking to people we had never met. We'd approach people and just start connecting. We'd been sent a ton of flowers, so of course we totally re-gifted many of them, showing up at our neighbors' doors with fresh bouquets.

Once, a dude was coughing up a storm when I poked my head in his room. "Hey, man, what's going on?" I said. "I'm Jon, and this is my wife, Annalise. What are you in for?"

Lung transplant. He'd been in for months and hadn't gotten out of bed—despite the urgings of his nurse. I noticed a photo of a kid on his nightstand. "That your grandson?" I asked. "He's waiting to hug you, my man. You gotta get up. This world needs you. The world ain't done with us yet."

Anni would chat up the visiting family members. Our job was

to bring joy to a shitty situation. "This sucks, huh?" I'd say as an icebreaker, before coaxing a smile.

We made friends. There were the sisters—one who was in for heart surgery, the other her caretaker—who Googled me. "I knew you were somebody," one said, "by the size of your calves."

There was my man Charlie Brown, another lung transplant. There were the gay guys, one of whom had undergone the exact same surgery as I had, who had recently adopted a son. We became friends and are still in touch today.

We all looked like shit. We'd pass each other going slo-mo in the hallway, but I'd say, "Better slow down there, Speed Racer," and I'd get a smile, and pretty soon there would be currents of smiles crossing one another in the air, and what had once been a downer of a culture became more upbeat. Every day, on our walks, people would open their doors and wait for us, just to shoot the shit.

One fellow patient was considerably older than me. One day, his door was open and I peeked my head in. He looked like he was having a bad day—fatigued, barely moving. "You look like shit!" I muttered, taking him by surprise.

He looked me up and down. "I still look better than you," he said, breaking into a smile.

"You wanna take a walk, grab a juice box, call it a day?" I said. Making it each day to the refrigerator at the end of the long hall-way on our floor for a juice box had become a daily ritual. "Me and you, we're gonna hang on the outside." He perked up, even joined Anni and me for part of a walk.

I'm not sharing this to pat myself on the back. Our walks were really for *me*. When I'd get a smile back, I'd feed off that energy. Knowing that others were looking up to me made *me* feel stronger. And I needed strength every damn day.

I'd struggle to get up each morning of my hospital stay. I'd grab my IV and the "suitcase" that was connected to the tubes coming out of my stomach and I'd shuffle my feet to the bathroom. "Don't close the door," Anni would call out, wanting to hear if I collapsed.

I'd leave it slightly ajar and look at the sad picture staring back at me in the mirror. I looked like crap. I'd lost a lot of weight. My eyes were sunken in and glazed over. The person looking back at me looked . . . *defeated*. Every morning.

I started calling these morning meetings with myself my daily pity parties. But then something happened. I'd look back at my reflection and tell that dude that it ain't over until the clock ticks down to zero. "You stand tall," I'd say to myself. "You hold your head high. You walk proud. You got this."

It felt like every moment in my life until now had been leading to these pep rallies in my hospital bathroom. I was talking to myself, not listening to myself. By the time Anni and I emerged from our room each day to fire up all our floor mates, I'd coached myself back into the guy Andy Reid was talking about: the captain of my ship.

Just before being discharged from the hospital, I looked at myself in the mirror one last time and the tears came gushing out. I resolved to never forget this feeling of appreciation. We—all of us—take too much for granted. "We alive," I said to myself. Anni and I walked the hall, hugging all our friends and getting their cell numbers.

And then it was time to go home. Big Dom was waiting for us out front behind the wheel of his GMC Denali. I gingerly got into the backseat—if the airbag up front deployed, it would crush my sternum and I'd be killed instantly.

Holding a pillow between my chest and the seat belt, I rolled the window down. Once we took off, I flashed back on a dinner I'd had years ago when I was a Buffalo Bill, with my teammate Brian Moorman and the captain of a nuclear submarine.

"You're on a submarine for up to nine months at a time without ever rising to the surface," I remember saying to the captain. "When you finally come up and walk on land, does that feel weird?"

He nodded. "On a submarine, you don't feel or see speed," he said. "But when you drive a car, you look out the window and the world passes you by at speed. When I get back in a car after a long voyage, the slowest of speeds feel so fast because I see the world pass me by for the first time in a long time."

Sure enough, in the back of Dom's car, it felt like we were going real fast, even though Dom might only have been cruising at thirty miles per hour. I closed my eyes, loving the feeling of the wind hitting my face.

How many car rides had I gone on in my lifetime? How many had I really been present for? There I sat, window rolled down, feeling the air on my face. Tears streamed down. From the front passenger seat, Anni turned around: "You okay?"

My eyes were still closed. "The wind is back beneath my wings," I said softly. I reached forward and put my hand on Anni's shoulder. "We alive, baby," I said, finally.

Back at our South Philly condo—thankfully, we'd not yet sold it—I was on a regimen of twenty-one pills a day. One—a beta-blocker—just made me veg out. Time stood still; I found myself dreamily staring at a wall all day.

Anni became my warden. I'd tell her to go to yoga, that I'd be okay alone for a couple of hours, and she'd just squeeze my hand and say, "I'm not leaving your side." We bought these amazing recliners—the Gladiator—from Bob's Furniture, one for the bedroom and one for the living room. I'd sleep in the recliner at night, next to the bed; Anni would lie on the very edge of the mattress closest to me, her hand on mine.

Not that she slept. Her anxiety was through the roof. When I'd shift positions in the night, she'd bolt upright. "What's the matter?" she'd say. "Are you all right?" She'd hold a mirror under my nose while I slept, making sure it fogged up.

Our first attempt to get out for a meal was an adventure. We drove a few blocks to Bar Amis, one of our favorite Italian restaurants. I was still walking slowly and could barely raise my voice above a hoarse whisper. We sat outside. Midway through the meal, I started coughing, which hurt like hell. I went back to the car, where I'd left my pillow. I sat there for a bit, hugging my pillow to my chest, calming down, mustering the strength to go back. Once I did, we paid the bill and got up to leave.

Other than our waiter, no one had said a word to us all night. No fans, no autograph seekers. It was like I was invisible in Philly for the first time in about a decade. Looking back, I know what the silence was about: it was like when I went back to school after my dad killed my mom. No one knows what to say, so they keep their distance.

We slowly made our way to our car. I was shuffling my feet and squeezing my pillow in pain, while Anni's arm went around me, helping me walk. That's when we heard it, like a scene out of a movie. At first it was a lone, slow clap. Then someone else joined. Then a third. In short order, everyone on that patio started slow-clapping as well. Anni and I looked at each other and slowly turned around to find everyone standing, looking at us, slow-clapping. Not one word was said. I put my fist in the air and smiled, trying to hold back the tears.

As we got into our car, someone shouted, "We love you, Jon! Eagle for life!" The tears started falling. Until this moment, I don't think Anni fully understood the relationship I had with the Philly fans. "I love you," she said, "and apparently so does everyone else around here."

As we drove away, gliding past the slow-clapping crowd, I rolled down my window and put my fist in the air. I didn't have the strength to say, "I love you"—I didn't have the strength to speak at all—but that's what I was feeling. The idea that I'd given my all to this city for so long, and now here were these complete strangers saying, "We got you," man, it makes me tear up even now.

I was still groggy a lot of the time, thanks to all the pills and the trauma my body had gone through. It was, therefore, the perfect time for Anni to strike. See, she'd always wanted a dog. Me? Not so much. You open the door, they run out. You gotta take 'em for walks and pick up their poop. Nothing against dogs or dog people; I just didn't want the responsibility of dog ownership.

But there I was, vegging out on the couch, all dosed up on meds and pain pills, when Anni put the laptop on my lap and showed me a photo of a goldendoodle. It was the cutest thing I had ever seen in my thirty-seven years. I started sobbing—remember, I was drugged up. "He's so cute," I blurted out, unable to take my eyes from the little guy.

"You want a dog?" Anni asked.

"No, I want *this* little guy," I whispered. "And I want to name him Saint to remind us of every day we're alive!"

Anni looked at me like she was wondering, *Who are you, and what have you done with Jon?* But through my tears, I saw it very clearly. "You're my angel and that little guy is my saint," I told her.

So we got Saint, and trained him to help me out as an ESA—emotional support animal—and service dog. Because I needed help for a while. And I just love him so freakin' much. He's the coolest dude in the world. He doesn't bark, he doesn't slobber. He's smart, he loves water, he brings the ball back when you throw it . . . and he just loves to hang out. He's pure . . . *joy*. We're inseparable. If you invite me somewhere but Saint ain't on your guest list, that's cool, I'm gonna pass.

Saint helped with my recovery, but he wasn't a cure-all. I found myself having to relearn everything I'd always preached. For the first time in my life, I was impatient and could be mean-spirited. I wouldn't just snap; I'd lose it. I punched holes in three doors, two kitchen cabinets, and Anni's car dashboard—all for no good reason.

When Anni observed after one of my snap-outs that "Everyone else gets the nice Jon," it hit home: I wasn't always treating the person who mattered most to me like I wanted to be treated. Anni understood that it was all part of my recovery—my hormones were raging due to the cow-tissue valve and the material of my new aorta. My body was still getting used to this trauma it had gone through, and it was messing with my psyche.

One night, Anni and I were watching the TV show *Wentworth* and there was a scene inside a twelve-step recovery meeting. It hit me: *Maybe this is how I need to approach what I'm going through: like I'm in AA. When I'm about to lose it, I need to acknowledge to myself what's going down.* There were no excuses. I'd just have to talk to myself louder and more often, and take it not day by day but minute by minute.

I talked to my friend William Taylor about what I was going through. He got it. He'd been in a terrible car accident; most of those in it had died, and he'd spent two years paralyzed before coming back to walk again. I'd tell him about my emotional struggles, and the raging hormones. "The way I'm acting," I said, "that's not me."

"Man," William said, "the fact that you see that and acknowledge that means you can correct it."

The mood swings and bouts of depression and anger would continue; what I could control was my response to them. It was tough, though. I behaved in ways I'm not proud of. Like the time, back now in Huntington Beach, when Saint and I were in a grocery store and an old-timer—dude must have been about seventy—let me have it for bringing a dog into a food store. "You should be ashamed of yourself," he said, getting up in my grill. "It's a disgrace to bring a dog into a food store. It's dirty."

I'm embarrassed to say I lost it on him. I put that seventy-year-old in a choke hold in the frozen-food section before it dawned on me what I was doing. Did I *want* to be like my dad? I let him go, the poor stunned bastard. "Don't talk shit about my dog," I blurted out, before calling for Saint and rushing to find Anni in the next aisle and stunning her. "Hey, uh, I just choked an old man in the freezer section, we should probably go," I said.

You're better than that, Jon, I'd tell myself. That really shook me. The more I thought about it, the more I thought to ask myself, *What would Saint do?* when anger or frustration or sadness welled up inside me. Saint is better behaved than most kids. When Anni or I say "place" to him—meaning, "stay"—he freezes. When I had that old guy pinned against the door in front of those frozen pizzas? Saint was looking up at me, his head slightly cocked. I could swear I knew what he was thinking: *Seriously? Chill out, dude.*

Yes, the weird stuff going on inside my body was making me more jumpy and angry. But *how* to deal with it was up to me. And the answer was right in front of me: be more like my man Saint.

My voice was still soft and shaky when Ellen invited me on her show not even eight weeks after the surgery. This time, it wasn't to perform magic, but rather to sit with her and tell my story. I went through it all: getting traded, learning I had a ticking time bomb inside my chest, finding the penny. My voice hoarse and choking with emotion, I showed a photo of Saint and professed my love for Anni, who was in the audience.

Ellen gave me the coolest gift: a doghouse for Saint made out of giant playing cards. I almost lost it. "Listen, you have free time now," Ellen said. "I want you to come back as often as you can. I want you here as much as possible. We're doing Twelve Days of Giveaways. Come back and help me with that."

And she meant it. Ellen is that person you see on TV. I love her life story, how she felt lost in her teens, how she feared coming out might ruin her career as an up-and-coming comic in the nineties. Turns out, she was *right* about that; the phone didn't ring for three years. But in that valley, she found purpose. She inspired others who saw in her story their struggle to live their truth.

Why did I feel Ellen and I were such kindred spirits? Because I felt like I'd known her. She may be tiny and not a world-class athlete, but she's not so different from any of the great leaders I shared a locker room with. She leads by putting others first. The best coaches or quarterbacks are the guys who call your number the very next play after you've fumbled the ball away. They're the first to say, "I believe in you"—and that belief becomes a self-fulfilling prophecy.

That's what Ellen did for me when she invited me to cohost the 12 Days of Giveaways segment with her, in which she gives away a massive amount of Christmas gifts to her audience.

There was just one problem. The short segment I'd just done with her left me with no voice for days. Turns out, losing your voice and vocal-cord damage is a frequent side effect of my surgery. So, leading up to our taping of 12 Days, I maintained a monklike silence for seventy-two hours—preserving my vocal cords. After the taping, I again needed days to get my voice and energy back.

After that, Ellen's producers started booking me regularly, and even eventually developed some set pieces for me, like "Cash at Your Dorenbos" and "Dollars from Dorenbos," in which Ellen directs me from the studio to surprise fans at home and give away tens of thousands of dollars.

We never really talked about it, but I think Ellen and I both understand that giving is really, at once, both a selfless *and* selfish act. It's selfish in that we do it to make ourselves feel better. Every time I've made someone else's day a bit brighter, it's put an extra bounce in *my* step.

Well, when Ellen invited me to cohost the 12 Days segment with her not two months after my surgery, I was on the receiving end of her giving. And it meant the world to me. Consider where I was in life. My football career was over; I'd just had open-heart surgery; I was out, like, more than $3 million. I didn't know what was next for me. It would have been easy to feel lost or aggrieved or depressed.

But I had Saint climbing all over me, I had Anni loving me through every day, and now I had Ellen giving me a place to go and perform as often as I could. It was a lifeline and a sign that— once again—I'd figure shit out, just like Ellen did despite her low moments a few decades ago. I would be okay.

Feel sorry for myself? *Puh-leeze.* There were too many good things happening. "We alive, baby," I'd begin and end every day saying to Anni—needing us both to hear the words.

CHAPTER SEVENTEEN

The Ring

A champion is someone who gets up, even when he can't.
—Jack Dempsey

Recovery is a funny thing. There isn't any one moment when you realize you're back to being you. Instead—like life itself—it's a process of fits and starts, of trial and error, of successes and failures. I worked to recapture my patience. I'd always lived my life looking at what's right in front of me with a sense of wide-eyed, childlike wonder. Now I had to consciously retrain myself to think that way.

When you do that, when you can't find your car keys and you say to yourself, *Isn't this interesting?* instead of cursing your bad luck through gritted teeth . . . suddenly the world becomes a kinder, gentler, more amusing place. But it's easier said than done. Getting to that state of wonder required some intensive self-coaching in the moment. *Calm down, Jon,* I'd say. Or: *You know this doesn't mean shit, right, Jon?*

Anni knew I was returning to me when she heard that old telltale sound coming from my hands, for hours on end. Just me and my fifty-two buddies. Ahhh, the echo of shuffling. The most soothing sound in the world. Saint would sack out, snoring, nearby; soon I moved beyond just shuffling. I started busting out some moves. Then I started writing them down.

Before I knew it, I was creating an entirely new show. One that had all the magic and comedy fun, but that also incorporated my life story. Mom would be a character in it, as would Dr. Bavaria; I'd make Anni and Saint magically appear, so they would *literally* be in the show. It would be a magic show that inspires and entertains. It would bring rock-star energy and it would feature the magic I learned throughout my journey in search of true happiness. In a way, the new show would be me, talking to my twelve-year-old self. And it would have three odd influences.

One was my man Scott Thompson, more commonly known as Carrot Top. His use of music and video clips make his shows stand out from all others. His isn't just a comedy show; it's a party.

Garth Brooks is also a buddy of mine; in fact, in Ellen's greenroom on that first appearance after my heart surgery, he toasted the fact that getting traded saved my life by saying, "Here's to unanswered prayers"—referencing his own song. How cool is that, Garth Brooks quoting himself to me?

Watching Garth Brooks in concert is an out-of-body experience. You see how much fun he is having, and how real he is. How passionate he is about his songs. That passion is contagious—it flows out into the crowd. He's only lightly scripted. He has his set list, but he tells stories and interacts with his fans off the cuff throughout. The audience member feels like he or she is just hanging out with a good friend. That's how I want my audience to feel.

Finally, there's Mike Tyson. His one-man show, directed by Spike Lee, gives us a guy who was once the most feared badass in the world being self-deprecating and vulnerable. He admits to things in his past that might make you think, *What a scumbag*, but then you're sitting there and you're *rooting* for him and liking him. When someone is that open and vulnerable, they become someone you want to get behind. The reality is that none of us are perfect; we've all made mistakes in life. Tyson's story proves that owning up to them, and coming back from them, are what people can relate to.

Once I'd fleshed out a new show with the music and energy of Carrot Top, the passion and connection to the audience of Garth Brooks, and the vulnerability and self-deprecation of Mike Tyson, Mooney dug it and got on the horn, booking gigs in Philly, Vegas, and points in between.

I still wasn't totally recovered. But I was itching to get out there in front of people and feed off their energy, even though my meds were still making me groggy. I hadn't even been watching football, though I was vaguely aware that the Eagles were winning.

Early in the season, just after I'd been released from the hospital, Jeffrey Lurie and his wife, Tina, had Anni and me over to dinner at their sick home on Philly's Main Line. The house sits on its own three-hole golf course; I had a perfectly cooked filet prepared by Jeff's private chef, and Anni had salmon.

We sat with the Luries for hours—I only had limited reserves of energy, and a multihour dinner was a challenge. My fatigue notwithstanding, I always felt better for having been in Jeffrey's company. I can be loud and a little rough around the edges, and he is always just the perfect gentleman. In all my years of working for the man, I'd never known him to raise his voice or be on a power trip.

I first got to know Jeff early on in my Eagles career during training camp at Lehigh University. It was August, and it was often a hundred degrees with excessive humidity. It was just plain miserable. Since I was a specialist, most of my time was spent just standing around, boiling. Offensive line coach Juan Castillo saw that I was doing precisely nothing and he told our starting right guard Todd Herremans, "Hey, Todd, that new snapper over there, he don't do much, does he? I'll get him to help with our drills." Soon I was being thrown around like a rag doll by the offensive line.

So I started to find any excuse I could to retreat into the equipment room. Not only to avoid drills that had nothing to do with my actual job, but also because the equipment room was . . . air-conditioned. *Nirvana.*

One day, while I was in there, hiding out, Jeff walked in. *Shit. Busted.* But Jeff wasn't there to rat me out. He told me how much he liked my magic, how happy he was that I was on the team. He'd lost his dad when he was nine years old, he said, and he could relate to the ways that magic and football had saved me. Sports had been a place of refuge and comfort for him, too. We bonded. From that moment on, Jeff was my guy. I think we sensed in each other a kindred spirit: two hurt kids who had to grow up too fast and too soon.

By the time we sat down to dinner at his Main Line home early in the 2017 season, we were just a couple of bros, hanging. At one point, Jeff's face took on a sheepish look. "You know, we're pretty good this year," he said.

"Of course you are," I replied, laughing. "You got rid of me. Of course you're killing it now."

We shared a laugh over this. It soon became apparent that Jeff was right: the Eagles were looking like one of those teams of destiny. You've seen them, teams whose sums add up to more than their parts. As I suspected, Carson Wentz was showing the world he was a first-class stud. The Eagles were coming up with big plays when they needed them, like kicker Jake Elliott's last-second sixty-one-yard field goal to beat the Giants, a win that made you wonder if the Birds' twelfth man was a certain deity who cared about football.

In Week 13, against the Los Angeles Rams, Carson went down with a torn ACL. Uh-oh. Just our luck, right, Philly? At the time of the injury, Carson had thrown thirty-three touchdown passes against just seven interceptions. The guy was putting up Tom Brady–like numbers, and carrying himself with Brady's kind of swagger, too.

By then, I was clear across the country in California, but even I could almost hear the Philly pain. *Not again. Just our luck.* There was no way the Eagles could win without their franchise player, right?

Wrong. The doubters hadn't stopped to consider ol' St. Nick. That would be backup quarterback Nick Foles, who has always had some measure of magic in him. I played with Nicky in 2013, when he put up one of the best quarterback years in recent memory: twenty-seven touchdown passes, just two interceptions.

I'd been a Nick Foles fan ever since. He looks the part of quarterback: Tall. Strong. Quick release. Plus, he and Carson were very similar; they could both run the same kind of offense. From the very first day Nick walked into the Eagles facility, players respected him. He studied. He always knew his assignments and responsibilities. He was kind and treated everyone with respect. And he balled out on game day.

Foles carried himself with a humility and a type of sensitivity I'd never felt from a quarterback before. A football team is a pack of alpha dogs, and the quarterback tends to be chief canine. Drew Bledsoe and Brett Favre come to mind. Off the field, they were down-to-earth good ol' boys, but on it they were throwback kind of leaders. They'd get in guys' faces and ferociously will their boys to victory.

But there's another type of leader. In his 1970 essay "The Servant as Leader," Robert K. Greenleaf coined the term "servant

211

leadership," and when you read up on the trend, you're likely to expect it to reference Foles. Not only isn't Nick standoffish; he carries himself like just one of the guys, and his every postgame comment seems to start with the pronoun "we" rather than "me." He talks about "staying in the moment" and is open about the self-doubt he experienced in 2015 when he went through a rough patch on the field and contemplated quitting the game. By being vulnerable in public, Foles actually leads, showing his guys that good things emerge *only* from struggle.

"A servant-leader focuses primarily on the growth and well-being of people and the communities to which they belong," Greenleaf wrote nearly fifty years ago. "While traditional leadership generally involves the accumulation and exercise of power by one at the 'top of the pyramid,' servant leadership is different. The servant-leader shares power, puts the needs of others first and helps people develop and perform as highly as possible."

In identifying the traits of a servant-leader, Greenleaf included listening, empathy, awareness, and persuasion. On the Eagles late-season run to the Super Bowl, Foles exhibited all of these traits at various times.

Anni and I went over to a neighbor's house to watch Foles and the Eagles take on the Minnesota Vikings in the NFC championship game. After Nick threw a five-yard touchdown pass to Alshon Jeffery early in the fourth quarter to put the Eagles up 38–7, I had to leave.

I don't mind saying, on the walk home, I was pretty bummed. *Are you serious? The first year I don't play and they go to the freakin' Super Bowl?* It was easy to feel sorry for myself, to wallow in all that I was about to miss out on.

"Jon, remember, if you play, you die," Anni said with a gentle smile. I'd been feeling robbed; all that work over eleven seasons, and *now* they go to the Super Bowl without me? But Anni snapped me out of it. She cut through that negative voice in my head and made me stop and think: *Life happens, man.* The difference between being happy and being depressed is how we deal with it. *I'd rather be alive. What a great day to be alive.*

"You're my Super Bowl, babe," I told her.

And then the damnedest thing happened. The cloud I'd been under lifted and I realized this wasn't all about me. My boys—my blood brothers I had gone to war with every Sunday for eleven years—they were going to the Super Bowl. Darren Sproles, Jason Peters, Brent Celek, Foles, Jason Kelce, Brandon Graham, and Donnie Jones were all going to the freakin' Super Bowl. And then I thought of staffers like "Cool as Shit" head of security Dom, and of the fans—was there a city more psyched to finally reach the NFL pinnacle?—and I started bursting with happiness for them. And then I realized that, hell, I was *one* of those fans now, so I was happy for me, too.

Meantime, I didn't know it, but Donnie had gone into Coach Pederson's office and they'd agreed that amid all the hoopla surrounding the team's first Super Bowl appearance in twenty-eight years, "something's missing."

"I know what it is: Magic Man," Donnie said.

"You think he'd come with us?" Doug asked.

They went to Jeff, who was thinking along the same lines. Within days, the call came from the Eagles: Would I join them for the Super Bowl? Uh, let me check my schedule . . . *hells, yeah!*

As a player, I always thought I'd be stressed out if I ever made it to a Super Bowl. But I never thought I'd be stressed at the Super Bowl because I had to be careful that, when in a crowd, I didn't get jostled or bumped into, lest my newly wired-shut sternum shifted out of line.

That's why, on the night before the big game, I found myself hanging back, waiting for all the other guests to clear out of the Minnesota art museum where Jeff Lurie had just hosted the party of all parties for about a hundred and fifty of his closest friends and family. "We're so happy to finally be going to the Super Bowl and representing the city of Philadelphia," Jeff had said to the crowd before unveiling a surprise. "Before we leave, I'd like to bring out a friend of mine to sing a couple of songs," and out came Sheryl Crow and her band. Anni and I were sitting, and rocking out, with Dr. Oz and Wall Street guru Jim Cramer—both huge Eagles fans.

Now, afterward, Anni and I waited while the others filed out. My balance still wasn't great, and I still walked slowly and carefully; this way, waiting for the place to empty, I could take my time leaving and not run the risk of colliding with anyone in the big crowd. We were the only two left in the room besides Jeff and Tina Lurie.

Jeff came up and gave me a light hug. I've never known him to cuss before, but he leaned in. "Hey, we're going to win this fucking thing," he said. "And when we do, you're going to get a ring. But not *just* a ring. You're going to get a *player's* ring, because you deserve it, for everything you did for this organization for so many years. The Super Bowl for you is living. And your ring will be a symbol for the way you've lived your life."

I ain't often speechless. I just leaned in and hugged my bro. As Jeff and Tina walked away, the tears started falling once again. Annie hugged and kissed me. "You always thought you'd only get a ring from playing, because you never wanted to coach," she said. "Isn't it funny how life works its way out? You aren't playing, and you sure as shit aren't coaching, but you might get that ring, after all."

The next afternoon, when the team was about to leave the hotel for the stadium, Mooney and I took a selfie with Foles and hung out with him for a few minutes, just talking about nothing. Once Foles got on the team bus, Mooney—a lifelong Eagles diehard—looked pale. "Dude," he said, "should I be worried? Foles was so relaxed, he looked like he was on his way to a yoga class."

That's Nick for you, I reassured him. The most Zen field general I've ever seen. Sure enough, a few hours later, St. Nick worked his magic against the favored New England Patriots. Everything felt right about the moment. I'd been coming back from my surgery—hell, I'd been coming back in one form or another since I was twelve years old—and now here was my team, which had been the underdog in each of its postseason games, modeling resilience for the world. As Anni and I made our way to the field to take part in the celebration, it just felt so *right*.

Anni and I took a photo with the trophy, and I hugged Donnie, Darren Sproles, and all my other brothers-in-arms. At one point, I looked up as confetti rained down on us. *So I didn't get to play, but this is what the confetti feels like.*

When Nick was named MVP and interviewed on the podium, hell if he didn't once again provide a life lesson in how to be a humble leader. How many other MVP interviews have featured the star saying something like, "I never stopped believing in myself" or some such *me, me, me*-ism? Not Nick.

"I think the big thing that helped me was knowing that I didn't have to be Superman," he said. "I have amazing teammates, amazing coaches around me. And all I had to do was just go play as hard as I could, and play for one another, and play for those guys."

Anni and I headed back to Philly for the parade. Something like three million fans turned out for it; Brian Dawkins and I waved to them from the alumni bus in the procession. Months later, the Eagles gave me my ring. That sucker is huge.

A lot of people were touched that I'd been given a ring, but there were also haters who weren't happy about it. It's true I didn't play a down for this team on the field. In fact, I've never even heard of a player who gets traded and is then given a Super Bowl ring by his former team.

But I've come to see it as symbolic of something bigger, something like what Jeff was getting at that night before the big game. After Mom's death, I had to learn how to lead with my heart. I had to learn to live my life like the most precious thing in it was my relationships. I like to think the Eagles gave me that ring because I treated everyone—teammates, coaches, staff, media—like they mattered, like each interaction was an end in itself, and not a means to an end. I don't need a ring to remind me I was good at football. My ring tells me I treated people the right way.

In the months after the Super Bowl whirlwind, my health gradually came back. So much so that I started performing across the country, often having to haul ass back to LA to tape *Ellen* shows. Things were good: Saint, Anni, and I would just hang out—we called our digs Casa Amor. We were basking in family life.

And then one day, shortly after we went off birth control, I walked through the front door and Anni handed me three pregnancy-test sticks. I thought she was asking me to open them for her to use, so I started to paw at them like an idiot. But they'd already been opened. And used.

"We're pregnant, honey," she said.

I jumped into her arms. *Me . . .* a dad. When we got our first sonogram, without saying a word, we showed it to Nonnie, who stared at it long and hard. "What is that?" she asked finally. "A picture of a puppy?"

"I hope not!" I said.

The closer we got to the arrival of Amaya Love Dorenbos—

that's right, Daddy's little girl—the more I thought of my own dad. It felt like everything in my life was coming together just as the universe had intended it to, but there was one relationship that never reached closure.

After it all—after the football, the magic, the heart scare, the Super Bowl, and the imminent arrival of Amaya—it was time to square the circle. It was time to come face-to-face with my father and tell him I forgave him.

CHAPTER EIGHTEEN

Closure

What was closure if not a clock? Not an end as everyone imagined, but a beginning.

—Celeste Chaney

The walls of the Safari Room restaurant in downtown Spokane, Washington, are filled with dead, stuffed animals staring right at you. A lion over here, a tiger over there. I feel their eyes beating down on me as I look around for my dad. Not here yet. I sidle up to the bar and order a Tito's and Seven.

I'd e-mailed him only a few weeks before. "It's been a long time," I wrote. "Not really sure what to say or what to write. I have no expectations. Want nothing from you. Just curious if you'd ever want to sit down sometime. Grab coffee."

Within a day, he had replied. "Hi," my dad wrote. "It is great to hear from you—I have been hoping and waiting for your time to be right. Would enjoy communicating with you and seeing you. Miss you greatly and don't know what to say either. Love Dad."

Now here I am, sipping a drink in the middle of the day, about to see my dad for the first time since our blowup of a visit twenty-six years ago at Walla Walla, when I was thirteen and dead-set on telling him what I felt. "Fuck *me*? Fuck *you*," he'd said.

I pull from my pocket a torn page from a notepad on which I'd written some notes to myself on the plane ride to Spokane. In sports, coaches talk all the time about "coaching you up," getting you in the right mind-set in order to achieve peak performance. Well, by continually reading my message to me, I am coaching myself up: *When walking in, have a heart full of love, kindness, and hope, and the swag that you are the biggest badass that has ever walked into whatever situation you're walking into . . . And you'll be fine.*

It's appropriate that I'm reviewing my game plan, because this feels like game time. *Bring it on.* Only Anni knows I'm here. I didn't tell Susan, Nonnie and Poppy, or Krissy. Why? Because this is for me. I don't want any judgment—whatever it might be. I am not here to start a relationship with my dad, or because I want answers about what happened that night, or to argue with or debate him. I am here, on one level, because I am curious: Who *are* you? What do you *look* like? And I am here to hear myself say what I've felt ever since I was twenty-two and talked to Mom that sunny day on Huntington Beach. *I forgive you.*

Let me tell you, I've spent my entire adult life thinking about forgiveness, and it's *deep*. Want to get healthy? Let go of whatever albatross has been weighing you down.

This isn't just a former football-playing meathead telling you this. There's a whole body of research out there that points to how transformative forgiveness is. A 2006 study by the Stanford Forgiveness Project, for example, held that forgiveness helps to reduce the stress we put on our immune and cardiovascular systems.

"Whenever you can't grieve and assimilate what has happened, you hold it in a certain way," Dr. Frederic Luskin, founder of the Stanford Forgiveness Project, told the *New York Times*. "If it's bitterness, you hold it with anger. If it's hopelessness, you hold it with despair. But both of those are psycho-physiological responses to an inability to cope, and they both do mental and physical damage."

According to Dr. Luskin, to get the full benefit of forgiveness, you need to keep in mind that the act of forgiving is for you, not the offender; it's about freeing *you*. It doesn't mean you have to like what your offender did, or become their friend. In order to forgive, the Stanford Forgiveness Project tells its clients, you first have to change "your story from that of a victim." Well, check, check, and check.

So here I am, sipping my vodka and Seven, eyes glued to the TV behind the bar—ESPN, natch. The doors to the hotel are in my line of vision; I recognize Dad as he enters the lobby. There he is, wearing a blue button-down shirt and khakis, walking toward me, hand outstretched. He is bald, save for wisps of hair combed back atop either ear, his complexion ruddy. A nervous smile creases his lips. We freeze-frame folks in our memory, so I am surprised that here is a seventy-year-old man walking my way. No doubt he didn't expect to see a grown man staring back at him.

"Wow, you're all grown up," he says as we shake hands.

"And you got old," I blurt out, both of us chuckling.

We grab a table and order Caesar salads and a margherita pizza. We make small talk. "I'm surprised you became a football player," he says. "You were always a baseball kid." I search his face and eyes for hints of me, but can find no resemblance. At one point, when he gets up to go to the bathroom, I look around the restaurant and wonder if, looking at us, the people around us see what we feel: that we are two strangers having lunch.

Dad tells stories about being in prison. Always smart and analytical, he became a jailhouse lawyer and helped inmates on their appeals. His volleyball team didn't lose a game in five years; "I miss the volleyball games," he says. I tell him that Krissy, with whom he hasn't been in touch, is doing well. "The world is a better place because Krissy's in it," I say.

When he went to jail, Dad says, he didn't care if he lived or died. Survival had been an accident. "I still don't give a shit," he says. I guess not caring is how he got through it all.

221

Today, Dad's life is simple, he says. Get this: when he was released in 2004, he tells me, a relative passed away and left him a sizable inheritance. He hasn't really worked since. He cares for his brother and rides his bike 150 miles a day.

Around this time, something interesting happens: all my complicated emotions fade away, as does our history. All the drama is . . . gone, at least for a few moments. All I am is a kid having lunch with his dad. Now, if you've had a functional upbringing, maybe you can't relate to this. Maybe you can't understand how any of it could fade away and how I could sit across from the man who took my mom from me.

But I'd never had this. I'd never had the opportunity to sit down with my dad and just shoot the shit. And, for this brief period of time, that's all I am doing, like I'd lived a normal, functional life and am just catching up with my old man over a few slices of pizza.

Of course, that simple, blissful feeling couldn't last. The longer I sit here listening to Dad's stories, the more I find myself unable to keep what had really happened in our lives at bay. I start to want to know about what led up to what happened that night. I know I'd said I wasn't here for answers, but the need to ask arises in me. I start to pepper him with questions, about him and Mom, about their life back then.

"Did you and Mom think about getting a divorce?" I ask at one point.

"We talked about seeing a counselor," he says, but then, each time I ask a question, he grows quiet and looks away for long silences, gazing at the TV screen behind the bar. Then, as if back on safe ground, he launches into some anti-Trump lecture or a speech about the need to decarcerate our prisons or legalize drugs.

Psychologists will tell you that many of those who have undergone trauma cope by, in effect, not dealing. They practice *avoidance* and *numbing*, putting their misdeeds and pain away somewhere deep, telling themselves they've moved on. I totally get it. You put your feelings in a bottle, seal it up, and bury it deep. Life moves on and you convince yourself you're at peace.

Dad says he had come to terms with what happened that night, and moved on. I get that, I tell him. And I mean it: if *I* had committed a horrible act, in order to continue my life, I suspect I'd have had to find a way to process what I'd done and find a way forward.

"It is what it is," Dad says, sighing, as I press him. At one point, he talks about Mom. "Your mom was the best mom ever," he says. "Some women go through an identity crisis. They have kids but want a career, too. All your mom wanted was to be a mom. She loved being a mom."

That gets me. My eyes water. I look around the restaurant, taking in all those stuffed animals staring at us from the walls. But there is only one elephant in the room. I ask again about what happened that night. Dad looks away, and speaks haltingly.

"You weren't there," he says. "I did what I felt I had to do. Obviously, I wish I would have done things differently. But I don't back down."

Seriously? Won't back down from a five-foot woman, tough guy? But then I catch myself. *You're here to listen, not debate.*

"You're right, Dad," I say. "I wasn't there. But you weren't there when I had to go to school and everybody was looking at me and talking about me 'cause I was the kid whose dad killed his mom."

He is looking at the TV; he drops his head to his chest and is quiet. Still looking down, he speaks softly. "You know what? I'm really sorry for the pain I've caused," he says, looking up. Now *his* eyes seem watery.

I don't get the feeling he is apologizing for killing Mom so much as for causing pain. And that's okay. Because I don't *need* to

223

hear him apologize. His ownership of what happened has no bearing on my journey to find peace, understanding, and happiness. I don't need his confession or his apology.

But I do need him to hear this—or, at least, I need to *say* it. "I forgive you for being lost, Dad," I say. He seems surprised, and nods.

We spend five hours having lunch, until it is time for me to head to the airport. Our waiter takes a photo of us, Dad with a beaming smile, holding the box with the leftover pizza slices. And there I am, looking stunned, thinking to myself, *Well, that just happened.*

On the way to the airport, I call Anni, the woman who had saved me in so many ways, the woman with whom I've built a safe, loving family life. I'll have a lot of processing to do in the coming days. But I already know I am glad to have sat down with my dad. It would have been easy not to, to just continue on with my life. But I know a few people who had been estranged from their dads; by the time they were ready to reach out to them, it was too late. I didn't want that to be me.

Besides, when has the easy way ever been the right way? By now, I know that when you do the hard thing, that's when you grow. And I'd just done the hard thing. I'd share all this with Anni, of course, but first I say something to her that I don't know I've ever said: "I just had lunch with my dad."

My teammates in NFL locker rooms might think I'm slightly off, but I've always believed in signs. Mom has always found a way to plant ideas in my head, whether it's signaling a direction for my act to follow on the eve of the *America's Got Talent* finale, or on that beach years ago, letting me know it was okay to forgive my dad.

Well, in the days and hours leading up to the meeting with my dad, I was searching the ground for stray pennies, looking for a sign from my mom that I was doing the right thing, and that she was with me. On my flight from Calgary to Spokane? No sign. Walking through the airport in Spokane? Still no sign. Walking through the parking lot, head down, to my rented Chevy Tahoe? Still no sign.

After our lunch, back at Spokane International Airport, I keep searching. "Are you shittin' me," I keep muttering to myself, head down yet again, trying to no avail to spot a random penny on the floor of first MVP Bar & Grill and then Spokane Tap Room. What, do they have a dedicated sweeper working the whole freakin' airport just to collect spare change off the floor?

Soon, it is time to board. I find my window seat—6A—and off we go. I put my headphones on and Johnny Cash's version of "You'll Never Walk Alone" speaks to me: *Walk on, walk on / With hope in your heart / And you'll never walk alone.* Just then the captain announces that we've reached our cruising altitude, and I raise the plastic window shade on my left and a burst of light shines through. I look out, squinting. We are peacefully in the clouds, gently gliding along.

As I look out on those clouds while ol' Johnny Cash's gravelly baritone assures me I'm not alone, a feeling comes over my whole body, like a comforting shiver. It is her. I *feel* it. This isn't me talking to her, as in the past, and this has nothing to do with convincing myself that a round piece of copper means something more than it does. Instead, this is me feeling her, deep in my soul. *Ahhh, there you are.* I feel such relief, closing my eyes and just letting Mom wash all over me. I feel her smile, that wide-eyed grin that gave off pure joy. I feel the *goodness* of her. I've gotten my sign. I know everything is going to be all right.

Two weeks later, tears streaming down my cheeks, there I am, holding a miracle weighing nine pounds and two ounces.

When Anni gives birth to Amaya, and I first hold my daughter, everything makes sense. The first words I ever speak to my daughter are to pledge to her that my whole purpose in this life is to make damn sure she can always have lunch with *her* dad, that she'll always know her dad is there for her, that she'll never look at her dad like I recently looked at mine and wonder: *Who the hell are you?*

On a beach some sixteen years ago, I first told my mom I had to forgive Dad if I wanted to become the man I thought she'd want me to be. Well, now here I am. I am Kathy Dorenbos's son. I am Annalise Dorenbos's husband. And I am Amaya Love Dorenbos's dad. I've become that man, Mom.

Acknowledgments

A lifetime in sports and entertainment has taught me that you never accomplish anything alone. This book was a labor of love for the all-star team I was blessed to have around me.

Jofie Ferrari-Adler and his team at Simon & Schuster's Avid Reader Press are world champions, and a pleasure to work with. Agent David Black is not only a Hall of Fame agent but also a source of life wisdom as well.

As you might imagine, this book was an emotional journey for me. Having Pro Bowl writer Larry Platt along for the ride gave me the strength and confidence to go the distance. As proud as I am about working with him, I'm even more proud of the friendship that has come from our partnership.

None of these pages would have come to fruition if Mike Tollin, a great friend, hadn't convinced me that my story could be both entertaining and inspirational.

I'm indebted to my man Tim Mooney, who was not only indispensable in shepherding this project to completion, but has also always been in my corner. And I shudder to think where I'd be without the wisdom over so many years of Dr. Kevin Elko. I also want to thank Patrick Bilow and Hannah Keyser for their tireless research and fact-checking as well as transcribing. Mike Vagnoni's Ambrosia Key West resort was the perfect tranquil setting to pen many of these pages. And Becky Roe, who was kind to a shell-shocked twelve-year-old when she prosecuted my dad, remains so to this day, having provided me with the trial transcript.

Finally, here's to Randy—keep rockin' and rollin', bro. As you might imagine, these pages are a love letter to the many characters who have so positively influenced my journey. I want to single out and address just a few: Annalise, Amaya, Susan, Nonnie and Poppy, and Krissy.

"If it's fun, it's never work," Hobie Alter, the surf and sailing entrepreneur, once said. "And if it's not fun, it will never work." You guys have made my life fun and our lives together sure ain't dull, huh?

I'm Jon Dorenbos. Peace out!

About the Author

Jon Dorenbos is a former professional football player, a world-class magician, and a motivational and corporate speaker. A special-teams long snapper, he played fourteen seasons in the NFL, appearing in the Pro Bowl twice. In his parallel career as a magician, he was a finalist on season 11 of *America's Got Talent* and appears frequently on *The Ellen DeGeneres Show*. He and his wife, Annalise, and daughter, Amaya, reside in Huntington Beach, California. For a schedule of performances or to book Jon as a speaker, go to JonDorenbos.com.

Larry Platt is the author of four books and coauthor of the *New York Times* bestselling memoir *Every Day I Fight*, the story of ESPN sportscaster Stuart Scott's epic cancer battle. He's the cofounder of *The Philadelphia Citizen*, a nonprofit news site, and the former editor of *Philadelphia* magazine and the *Philadelphia Daily News*. He can be reached at LarryPlatt.net.